GUINNESS WORLD RECORDS
Baffling Bodies

by Vicky Shiotsu and Shirley Pearson

D1518891

Carson-Dellosa Publishing LLC
Greensboro, North Carolina

Credits

Content Editor: Christine Schwab
Copy Editor: Julie B. Killian
Layout and Cover Design: Van Harris

Carson-Dellosa Publishing LLC
PO Box 35665
Greensboro, NC 27425 USA
www.carsondellosa.com

ISBN 978-1-60996-463-4
01-335111151

TABLE OF CONTENTS

SETTING GUINNESS WORLD RECORDS RECORDS

Guinness World Records accomplishments are facts or events that belong in one of eight categories:

- Human Body
- Amazing Feats
- Natural World
- Science and Technology
- Arts and Media
- Modern Technology
- Travel and Transport
- Sports and Games

Some records are new because they are exciting and involve events that have never been attempted before. People with unique talents or features are also permitted to become record setters. However, many of the records are already established, and people try to find records that they can break. One record holder, Ashrita Furman, has broken or set more than 300 records since 1979.

Guinness World Records receives more than 60,000 requests each year. Record setters and breakers must apply first so that their attempts are official. The organization sets guidelines for each event to make sure that it can be properly measured. Guinness World Records also makes sure that all record breakers follow the same steps so that each participant gets an equal chance. Professional judges make sure that the guidelines are followed correctly and measured accurately. However, the guidelines may designate other community members who can serve as judges to witness an event. Once the record attempt is approved, the participant gets a framed certificate. The person's name may also be included in the yearly publication or on the Guinness World Records Web site at *www.guinnessworldrecords.com*.

BE A RECORD BREAKER!

Hey, kids!

Tubby is a Labrador retriever that collected and recycled about 26,000 plastic bottles from his daily walks. Rob Williams (USA) made a sandwich with his feet in less than two minutes. Tiana Walton (UK) placed 27 gloves on one hand at one time. Aaron Fotheringham (USA) landed the first wheelchair backflip. The Heaviest Pumpkin ever weighed 1,725 pounds (782.45 kg). And Rosi, the Heaviest Spider ever, is larger than a dinner plate. What do all of these stories have in common? They are Guinness World Records records!

A world record is an amazing achievement that is a fact. It can be a skill someone has, such as being able to blow the largest bubble gum bubble. It can be an interesting fact from nature, such as which bird is the smelliest bird. Guinness World Records has judges who set rules to make sure that all record setters and record breakers follow the same steps. Then, the adjudicators (judges) count, weigh, measure, or compare to make sure that the achievement is the greatest in the world.

So, can you be a Guinness World Records record breaker? If you can run, hop, toss, or even race with an egg on a spoon, you just might see your name on a Guinness World Records Certificate someday. With the help of an adult, visit *www.guinnessworldrecords.com*. There you will find a world of exciting records to explore—and maybe break!

 The Carson-Dellosa Team

This Nose Really Blows!

Most Balloons Inflated by the Nose in Three Minutes
March 3, 2010

Some people are good at blowing up balloons. Andrew Dahl (USA) is one of them. But, he doesn't use his mouth as most people do. Instead, he uses his nose! In 2010, Dahl set a record for the Most Balloons Inflated by the Nose in Three Minutes. He blew up 23. That's more than seven balloons per minute!

How did Dahl start blowing up balloons with his nose? When he was seven, he grew bored while waiting in his family's car. He picked up a balloon and began to play with it. He discovered that he could use his nose to blow up the balloon. His dad thought it was a cool trick, and today many people would agree!

● Write the numbers 1 to 9 on the balloons so that the sum of the numbers on the outer triangle is double the sum of the numbers on the inner triangle. Also, the three numbers on each side of the outer triangle must have the same sum. Some numbers have been filled in for you.

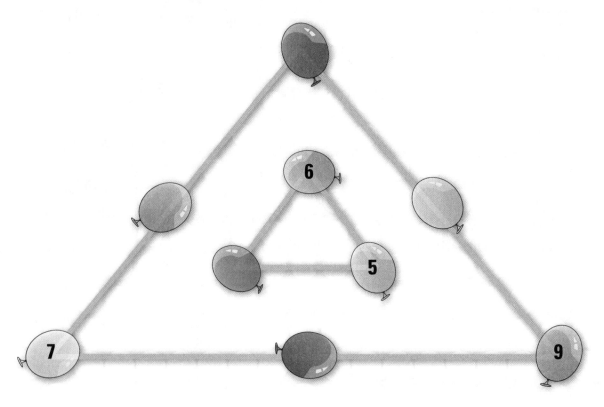

CD-104546

What a Tall Kid!

Tallest Teenager Living

Brenden Adams (USA) seemed like a regular kid when he was born, weighing 7 pounds (3.17 kg) at birth. That's the same size as many babies born in the United States. Then, Brenden started to grow and grow. By the time he was in elementary school, he was already as tall as an adult! Today, he is 7 feet 4 inches (2.24 m) tall. He holds the record for the Tallest Teenager Living.

Because Brenden is so tall, his parents had a house built to fit his height. The doors are a lot taller than those in other homes. The ceilings are high too. The house makes life a lot easier for Brenden. He can move around his home without bumping his head everywhere he goes!

● Learn more about Brenden Adams. First, solve the problems. Then, write the answers on the lines to complete the sentences.

1. 25 + 18 – 20 – 4

At birth, Brenden was a little more than _____ inches long.

2. 37 – 16 – 19 + 2

When Brenden was _____ years old, he was the size of an eight-year-old.

3. 42 – 29 + 3 – 8

When Brenden was _____ years old, he was the size of an adult.

4. 35 + 6 – 37 + 8

When Brenden was _____ years old, he was more than 7 feet tall.

CD-104546

Face Painting Fun

Most Faces Painted in an Hour by an Individual
September 1, 2007

Who do you think has more fun with face paint—the person being painted or the person doing the painting? According to Gary Cole (USA), it is probably a tie! Cole still gets a thrill from watching children smile when they see their painted faces in the mirror. Cole owns a face-painting company. He has painted thousands of faces. He has also trained thousands of face painters.

In 2007, Cole had a blast while breaking the world record for the Most Faces Painted in an Hour by an Individual. He almost tripled the previous record. Cole painted an amazing 217 full-face designs. He painted each face using three colors, and each face was different. The greatest challenge that day, Cole said, was coming up with enough children to paint. He and another face painter were competing for the record title at a shopping mall in Scotland. Between the two artists, they painted more than 400 faces. The children were kept busy too. As soon as each child had one design painted on her face, she was photographed, washed, and sent back for another. Cole thinks that the children should have won awards too!

● Below is a numbered grid of face paint colors. Beside each selection, describe the type of face design you would paint using just those colors. Then, write your own groups of colors for the last two numbers in the grid.

1. red/white/blue		**5.** green/blue	
2. orange/black		**6.** brown/white	
3. yellow/blue		**7.**	
4. white/black/pink		**8.**	

CD-104546

Hairiest Family

Have you ever had a bad hair day? Don't complain to the Ramos Gomez family of Mexico. Nineteen members of the family don't just have hair on their heads. They have thick hair all over their bodies. People with this condition used to be called "werewolves." Now, Larry and Danny Ramos Gomez are called "Wolf Boys" at the circus where they work. Larry and Danny are normal in every other way, except for their hair. No known cure exists for *hypertrichosis*, or "werewolf syndrome." But, scientists are studying the Ramos Gomez family in hopes of finding one.

● It might be hard to get to know a person under all that hair. It is the same for the following sentences. The letters from the word *hair* have been added everywhere. Cross out the letters *h, a, i,* and *r* to discover something that Danny Ramos Gomez said. Then, write the words on the lines. (Hint: If you see double *hair* letters together [*hh, aa, ii, or rr*], just remove one of the letters.)

Apheiopale iwahho aahrrie hdiifafeirrhaent isthiirll ihhiaave adiighiniitry

_____ _____ _____ _____ _____ ____ _____.

Iiaamah aveirrahy iprriohud rthor rabe rwrihho Iih raamah

____ ____ _____ _____ ____ ____ ____ ____.

Love Soars to New Heights

Tallest Married Couple (Living)
November 18, 2010

Laurie and Wayne Hallquist (both USA) must have turned heads on their wedding day. That's because they are the world's Tallest Married Couple (Living). Laurie is almost 6 feet 6 inches (1.98 m) tall. Wayne stands about 6 feet 10 inches (2.08 m). Together their heights total 13 feet 4 inches (4.06 m)!

The two married in 2003. With their heights, they seemed made for each other! The couple contacted Guinness World Records after learning that they had a chance at winning a record title. When they won in 2010, they were thrilled. Laurie and Wayne were truly "on top" of the world!

● The combined heights of the Hallquists is 13 feet 4 inches, or 160 inches. Fill in the missing numbers on the wedding cake until you reach 160 at the top. (Hint: Look for the pattern.)

CD-104546

Bubble Gum Granny

Largest Bubble Gum Bubble Blown with the Nose
November 10, 2000

You know how to blow a bubble gum bubble, right? Joyce Samuels (USA) does too. She loves to chew gum and blow bubbles. But, Bubble Gum Granny doesn't just blow bubbles with her mouth. She uses her nose! Samuels chews the gum for about an hour. Then, she flattens it across the bottom of her nose and sticks the edges to her cheeks. After that, she blows, and blows, and blows. Her largest bubbles have measured as big as 11 inches (27.94 cm) in diameter.

People have been chewing some sort of "gum" for centuries. But, bubble gum wasn't invented until about 100 years ago. A special gum from the sapodilla tree was the trick ingredient behind the first big, beautiful bubbles ever blown.

● Starting with the phrase *BUBBLE GUM,* follow the directions to discover the name of the secret trick ingredient.

B U B B L E   G U M

1. Remove all of the *B*'s.

_____

2. Replace all of the *U*'s with *C*'s.

_____

3. Move the last three letters, in order, to the beginning.

_____

4. Reverse the first two letters.

_____

5. Replace all of the *G*'s with the next letter in the alphabet.

_____

6. Change the third consonant in the word to the vowel that means "ME."

_____

A Balancing Act

Heaviest Car Balanced on the Head
May 24, 1999

Have you ever balanced an object on your head? John Evans (UK) has. Evans entertains people. In his act, he balances very heavy objects on his head. One time, it was 101 bricks. Another time, it was 429 full soft drink cans. Evans has even balanced people on his head!

In 1999, Evans set a record for the Heaviest Car Balanced on the Head. The car was a gutted MINI Cooper. It weighed 352 pounds (160 kg). Evans kept the car on his head for 33 seconds. Evans really is someone who has to "use his head"!

● Below are the names of six children and their weights. Which four children's weights would equal the weight of the car that John Evans balanced on his head?

Tony

77 pounds

Amira

65 pounds

Kevin

92 pounds

Emma

81 pounds

Carlos

94 pounds

Janelle

89 pounds

The four children are _____ , _____, _____ ,

and _____ .

CD-104546

Talk, Talk, Talk

Fastest Talker
August 30, 1995

Sean Shannon (Canada) can talk a lot. When he speaks, he can squeeze a lot of words into just a few seconds. Shannon is the world's Fastest Talker. In 1995, he recited a famous speech from a Shakespearean play called *Hamlet*. The speech begins, "To be or not to be." It contains 260 words. Shannon spoke all of the words in less than 24 seconds. That's the same as 655 words per minute. That's almost 11 words per second!

People who talk fast for a living cannot even talk as fast as Shannon can. For example, people who work at auctions speak up to 400 words per minute. Still, Shannon thinks he may try to beat his own record. He says he would like to get his speed up to 660 words per minute!

● About how fast do people usually speak? To find out, read the clues. Cross out the numbers that match the sums below. Then, complete the sentence at the bottom of the page with the number that is left.

- 300 + 60
- 200 + 40
- 400 + 10
- 500 + 80
- 100 + 30
- 400 + 70
- 200 + 90
- 100 + 90
- 300 + 20
- 500 + 30
- 100 + 10
- 300 + 70

110	130	150
190	240	290
320	360	370
410	470	530
	580	

Most people speak about _____ words per minute.

Tissue, Please!

Longest Spaghetti Ejected from the Nose
December 16, 1998

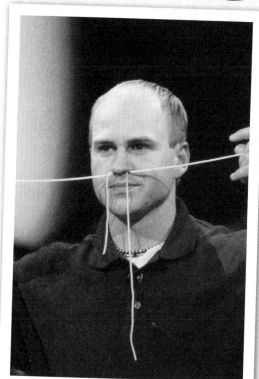

Your nose is the opening of a tunnel through your head. The tunnel runs from your nostrils to the top of your throat. Breathing drives air in and out. Sneezing just drives air out. The tunnel is called the nasal cavity. Some people have large nasal cavities. Kevin Cole (USA) is one of those people. Cole can blow food out of his nose. To achieve this record, Cole placed a cooked spaghetti noodle in his mouth. But, he didn't swallow it. Instead, he used his tongue to push the noodle up into his nasal cavity, and then—*achoo*!—he sneezed it out. The 7.5-inch (19.1-cm) spaghetti noodle dangled from his nostril. Meatballs, anyone?

● Because we use our noses for breathing, shoving things such as food into them is not a good idea. The words **spaghetti**, **noodle**, and **meatball** have something in common besides making a great meal. They each contain consecutive identical letters. Below are the names of several other foods that you should not shove up your nose. Each word also contains consecutive identical letters. Use the clues to complete the words.

___ ___ dd ___ ___ ___ a creamy dessert	___ oo ___ ___ ___ a treat you grab from a jar
___ ___ ee ___ ___ mozzarella or cheddar	___ pp ___ ___ Granny Smith or red delicious
___ ee ___ a pinkish-red root vegetable	___ ___ rr ___ ___ an orange vegetable that rabbits like
___ ___ ff ___ ___ a square or round breakfast food, served with syrup	___ ___ rr ___ ___ ___ ___ hot breakfast cereal eaten by the Three Bears
___ gg something laid by a chicken	___ ___ tt ___ ___ something you spread on toast
___ ___ ll ___ something you eat with peanut butter	___ ___ tt ___ ___ ___ main part of a salad

The Push-Up King

Most Push-Ups with One Arm, Using the Back of the Hand, in One Hour
November 8, 2008

What is the cheapest way to get fit? If you ask Doug Pruden (Canada), he is sure to answer, "By doing push-ups." No equipment or gym is needed—just a floor! Pruden should know. He is the world's Push-Up King. In 2008, Pruden bested his own record by doing the most difficult push-up of all: the one-armed, back-of-the-hand push-up. In one hour, he completed 1,025 of these tricky exercises. His arm strength is amazing!

Pruden has to follow certain rules when doing one-armed, back-of-the-hand push-ups. He must push up with the same arm for all push-ups. The back of his hand must stay flat on the floor the whole time. Ouch! And, his body must remain straight. No bending at the knees or waist is allowed. He must lower his body until his elbow is completely bent. And, his body must stay even with the ground. Then, he must raise himself until his arm is straight. He does this again and again. As Pruden says, "World records are painful but fun when you break them in the end!"

● *Push up* is a two-word phrase. To the right is a list of other two-word phrases. The opposites of these phrases can be found in the word bank. For each phrase, write the opposite two-word phrase in the spaces provided.

push up	pull	down
after vacation		
ask now		
empty mine		
laugh quietly		
open quickly		
run over		
smile frequently		
stand high		
take few		
teach badly		
wet day		
young woman		

Word Bank

answer	man
before	many
close	night
cry	old
dry	seldom
fill	sit
frown	slowly
give	under
later	walk
learn	well
loudly	work
low	yours

A Sticky Record

Most Self-Stick Notes on the Body
April 24, 2010

Self-stick notes are handy for writing short reminder notes. But, what about using them to set a world record? That's what two young men did in Sweden. Daniel Olofsson and Martin Holmkvist (both Sweden) stuck notes all over Dennis Persson. The two stuck on green notes and pink notes. They stuck on yellow notes and orange notes. They didn't stop until they had covered Persson with 286 notes. That was enough to win the record for the Most Self-Stick Notes on the Body. Hopefully, the record will "stick around" for a long time!

● How long did it take Olofsson and Holmkvist to place 286 self-stick notes on Persson's body? To find out, follow the directions and cross out the notes below. Then, look at the remaining letters. Write them in order on the lines.

- Cross out the notes with numbers that equal 780 when rounded to the nearest ten.

775	682	579	771	633
o	f	n	i	t

- Cross out the notes with numbers that equal 600 when rounded to the nearest hundred.

512	1,669	781	1,584	999
v	e	d	m	a

- Cross out the notes with numbers that equal 1,000 when rounded to the nearest thousand.

1,780	624	1,907	705	1,243
i	y	n	u	w

784	1,720	1,009	1,561	694
a	t	k	e	s

It took Olofsson and Holmkvist __ __ __ __ __ __ __ __ __ __ __ to put all of the self-stick notes on Persson.

CD-104546

A Prize-Winning Beard

Longest Beard on a Living Male
March 4, 2010

Sarwan Singh (Canada) is a Sikh, a member of a religious group founded in India. Because of his beliefs, he has never cut his beard. His beard has grown to become the Longest Beard on a Living Male. It measures 7 feet 9 inches (2.4 m) long!

Looking at Singh, you would never know his beard is that long. That's because he keeps it rolled and tied neatly just a few inches below his chin. Singh calls his beard a source of pride. To keep it clean, he washes it with water every day. He also shampoos it twice a week. He says his beard is more important to him than any other part of his body.

- Mr. Lee has a beard. Like Singh, he shampoos it every week. Suppose Mr. Lee shampoos his beard every three days. Look at the calendar and answer the questions.

1. Mr. Lee shampoos his beard on the first Wednesday of the month. On what date will he shampoo his beard on a Wednesday again? _____

2. On the calendar, cross out the days when Mr. Lee will shampoo his beard. How many times will he shampoo it this month? _____

3. Find the pattern. If Mr. Lee shampoos his beard on a certain day of the week, how many days later will he shampoo it on that day again?

_____

Sunday	Monday	Tuesday	Wednesday	Thursday	Friday	Saturday
		1	2	3	4	5
6	7	8	9	10	11	12
13	14	15	16	17	18	19
20	21	22	23	24	25	26
27	28	29	30			

CD-104546

Dancing Grandma

Oldest Acrobatic Salsa Dancer (Female)
March 4, 2010

Age is just a number. That's what Sarah "Paddy" Jones (UK) believes. At age 75, Jones was declared the Oldest Acrobatic Salsa Dancer (Female) in the world. So, how good is she? She is good enough to win a Spanish talent show and tour the world! "I just love dancing," she says. "When the music starts, I find it hard to keep still." Jones only learned to salsa dance when she retired to Spain at age 70. She actually danced professionally as a young girl but stopped to become a dental nurse when she got married. She now has four children and seven grandchildren.

It is not a coincidence that the word *salsa* means "hot sauce" in Spanish. Dancing the salsa is hot work for both partners! Their feet and hips are continuously moving. Jones specializes in acrobatic salsa dance. Her feet are not always on the ground. Her partner lifts, slides, and practically throws her around the dance floor. "I'm sure it keeps me young," Jones says. "As long as I can keep it up, we [she and her partner] will still do it."

● Acrobatic salsa is just one of hundreds of different dance styles. Jones ended up dancing the salsa because she couldn't find a convenient flamenco class. The word bank on the following page contains the names of several dance styles. These words appear either vertically or horizontally in the puzzle. The unused puzzle letters, in order from top to bottom and left to right, will spell the word used when referring to huge salsa dance parties.

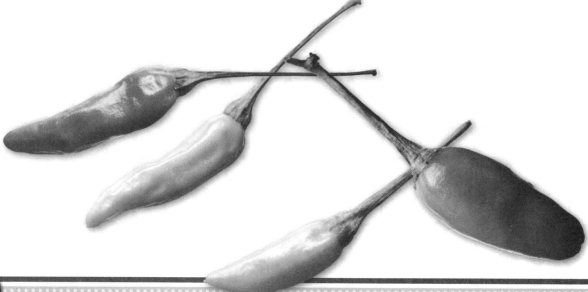

CD-104546

Word Bank

ballet	cha-cha	gumboot	jazz	polka	waltz
Bollywood	flamenco	hip-hop	jive	rumba	
break dance	fox-trot	hula	merengue	tango	

```
B   O   L   L   Y   W   O   O   D   F

R   U   M   B   A   A   C   O   C   L

E   H   E   P   O   L   K   A   H   A

A   I   R   N   B   T   G   F   A   M

K   P   E   J   A   Z   Z   O   C   E

D   H   N   J   L   T   H   X   H   N

A   O   G   I   L   A   U   T   A   C

N   P   U   V   E   N   L   R   R   O

C   E   E   E   T   G   A   O   S   S

E   G   U   M   B   O   O   T   E   S
```

Huge salsa dance parties are called ___ __ __ __ __ __ __ __ __ __ __ __ .

The Case of the "Nosy" Typist

Fastest Time to Type Using the Nose
November 16, 2008

People who spend much of their workdays typing may reach speeds of 50 to 60 words per minute. That's about a third of a typewritten page. These people use their fingers to type. The keyboard is perfectly designed for the human hand. Neeta (India) is also a very fast typist. In fact, she holds the 2008 Guinness World Records record for typing quickly. In one minute, 33 seconds, Neeta typed 103 characters. That's about 18 words. This means that Neeta's typing speed was around 12 words per minute. So, how did that earn her a world record? Neeta didn't type using her fingers. She typed using her nose!

● Use the clues to complete the crossword puzzle.

ACROSS

3. The English alphabet has 26 of these.

6. Opposite of slowest

7. Neeta's native country

8. The letters on the keyboard

DOWN

1. WPM is short for "_____ per minute."

2. Neeta's record was one _____, 33 seconds.

4. She holds a Guinness World Records _____.

5. Many typing teachers use the sentence "The quick brown fox jumps over the lazy dog" because it contains all of the letters of the _____.

6. Most people use these to type.

CD-104546

Body of Art

Most Tattooed Person

Lucky Diamond Rich (Australia) has many skills. He rides unicycles. He juggles chain saws. He even swallows swords. But, those acts are not what he is most known for. Rather, he has a body that makes people take a second look. Rich holds the record for being the Most Tattooed Person in the world. He has spent more than 1,000 hours getting his body tattooed!

Rich has worked with hundreds of tattoo artists. At first, he had colorful designs tattooed all over his body. Later, he added a covering of black ink. After that, he added white designs on top of the black. Rich is a walking body of art. Even the inside of his ears and the skin between his toes are tattooed!

● **Four children went to the toy store to buy temporary tattoos. Write what they bought. Use the clues and the table to help you.**

• Justin got the butterfly or the dinosaur.

• Lee got the dog or the unicorn.

• Kori did not get a four-legged creature.

• Tracy got the unicorn or the butterfly.

Justin _____

Lee _____

Kori _____

Tracy _____

	butterfly	dog	unicorn	dinosaur
Justin				
Lee				
Kori				
Tracy				

The Ironman

Farthest Distance to Pull a Bus with the Hair (Male)
November 11, 2009

When you see a bus, you probably think of sitting in the seat as a passenger or sitting up front as the driver. When Manjit Singh (UK) sees a bus, he probably thinks, "How far can I pull this thing?" Singh's nickname is the Ironman. He holds many world records for strength. In 2009, he pulled a double-decker bus a distance of 69.55 feet (21.2 m). And, he didn't use his arms. He used his hair! Singh hooked a long strap to the bus. Then, he attached a heavy screw to his ponytail. He fastened the other end of the strap to the screw and pulled. It's not just strength that

helps the Ironman break records. He spends a lot of time meditating. He also spends a lot of time at the gym.

● Manjit Singh has also set other records for important reasons. To figure out the missing words in the record descriptions below, unscramble the boxed letters in each attached sentence. Then, write the words on the lines.

Pulled a double-decker bus with his ____ ____ ____ ____

Pulled a double-decker bus with his ____ ____ ____ ____ ____

Pulled a double-decker bus with ____ ____ ____

____ ____ ____ ____

Singh [e]njoys b[r]e[a]king record[s].

[I]t h[e]lps [h]im raise mon[e]y for chari[t]y.

His fav[o]rite charity rais[e]s money to [h]elp chil[d]re[n] in Ind[a] become involved i[n] sports.

Action Hero

Shortest Stuntman
October 20, 2003

Kiran Shah (UK) is an actor and a stuntman. He holds the record for the world's Shortest Stuntman. Shah stands 4 feet 1.7 inches (1 m 26.3 cm). That's about 1 foot (0.3 m) shorter than the height of many grown adults!

Although he is small in size, Shah has made a big name for himself in films. Since 1976, he has appeared in more than 50 movies. He has performed stunts in many of them. In his second film, he had to fall from a height of 30 feet (9.1 m). That's as high as a three-story building! Shah isn't bothered by heights though. He also loves doing stunts. He says, "I love any kind of action."

● **Imagine that some fans of Kiran Shah went to see one of his movies. The movie tickets cost $10.00 for adults and $7.00 for children. Read the clues. Then, write the number of adults and children who were in each group.**

1. A group of 6 people went to the morning show. The cost was $51.00.

   adults _____ children _____

2. A group of 8 people went to see Shah's movie at noon. The cost was $65.00.

   adults_____ children _____

3. A group of 10 people bought tickets for the late-afternoon show. The cost was $82.00.

   adults _____ children _____

A Steady Hand

Most Eggs Held in the Hand
March 21, 2009

You have probably held one egg in your hand, right? Maybe you have even held two or three. But, have you ever held more than 20 in one hand at one time? Zachery George (USA) did! He holds the record for the Most Eggs Held in the Hand. In 2009, he placed 24 eggs in one hand and held them for 40 seconds. He beat the old record of 20 eggs held for 10 seconds.

George is happy about his record, but he is not done yet. He wants to try setting more world records with his hands!

● Shane, Tyesha, and Kelly have a large basket of eggs. They will try holding eggs in one hand like Zachery George did. Read the clues to answer the questions below.

First, Shane takes half of the eggs that are in the basket.

Next, Tyesha looks at the eggs that are left in the basket and takes half of them.

After that, Kelly looks at the eggs that are left and takes half of them.

Now, 4 eggs are left in the basket.

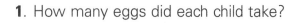

1. How many eggs did each child take?

Shane _____

Tyesha _____

Kelly _____

2. How many eggs were in the basket before the children took some?

_____

Table Manners

Loudest Burp by a Male
June 16, 2009

"Excuse me" is what a polite person says after burping. Paul Hunn (UK) is polite. But, when he burps, he probably says, "Do you want me to do it again?" That's because Hunn's burps are the loudest in the world. He set the record with a burp that measured 109.9 decibels. That's about as loud as a snowmobile! So, how does he burp so loudly? Hunn performs on an empty stomach. That leaves more space for air and gas to build up. As he feels air rising to his throat, he opens his mouth and lets it roar. Hunn's talent has taken him around the world. He jokes that when he flies, his seatmates always want to switch seats once they find out why he is famous! Despite his loud belches, Hunn remembers his manners. He gives special thanks to his family for putting up with his "disgusting habit."

● Everyone burps, and every language has its own expression for the phrase **excuse me**. On the left is a list of languages and their words for *burp*. Match the apology on the right with its correct language by filling in the blanks.

(English)	burp
(Filipino)	dighay
(French)	roter
(German)	rülpsen
(Hungarian)	böfögtet
(Indonesian)	atop
(Italian)	rutto
(Japanese)	geppu
(Maltese)	tifwiq
(Norwegian)	rap
(Portuguese)	arroto

Excuse me (E n g l i s h)

Elnézést (__ __ __ __ **a** __ __ __ __)

Entschuldigen sie bitte (__ **e** __ __ __ __)

Excusez-moi (__ __ **e** __ __ __)

Mi perdoni (__ __ __ __ __ __ **a** __)

Patawad po (__ __ __ **i** __ __ __ __)

Perdoe me (__ __ __ __ __ __ __ __ **e** __ __)

Permisi (__ __ __ __ __ __ __ __ **i** __ __)

Shitsurei shimashita (__ __ __ __ __ __ **e** __ __)

Skuzi (__ **a** __ __ __ __ __)

Unnskyld meg (__ __ __ __ __ **e** __ __ __ __)

CD-104546

May I Use Your Floss?

Most People Flossing on the Same Length of Floss
March 19, 2004

You know that flossing helps keep your teeth clean. But, did you know that flossing is also a Guinness World Records event? In 2004, children and adults from two North Carolina schools showed off their flossing skills. They won the record for the Most People Flossing on the Same Length of Floss.

Students, parents, and teachers took part in the event. They were from Lake Norman Elementary School and Brawley Middle School (USA). All 1,470 of them met at Lake Norman Elementary. They lined up around the school. Then, they started flossing their teeth. Everyone used a single line of dental floss. The floss measured 6,000 feet (1,828.8 m). It stretched more than a mile (1.6 km) long!

● Imagine that your school wants to have a flossing event too. A teacher is making number cards for the students to wear to help her keep track of the children. Answer the questions below.

1. Suppose the teacher writes the numbers 1 to 100 on the cards. Which digit would be written the most often? (The digits are 1, 2, 3, 4, 5, 6, 7, 8, 9, and 0.) _____ How many times would the teacher write that digit? _____

2. Which digit would be written the least? _____ How many times would the teacher write that digit? _____

That's a Mouthful!

Most Rattlesnakes Held in the Mouth
December 20, 2008

Jackie Bibby (USA) is the Texas Snake Man. Bibby is a poisonous snake expert. While most people run away from rattlesnakes, Bibby does exactly the opposite.

● The following paragraph gives more information about the Texas Snake Man. Some of the words have been replaced by words that mean exactly the opposite. Cross out these opposite words. Using the word bank, write the correct words in the spaces provided.

Bibby **removes** ———— rattlesnakes in his bathtub.

He puts them in his sleeping bag. He even puts them **outside** ———————— his mouth. Bibby holds the

record for the **Least** ———— Rattlesnakes Held in the Mouth. In 2008, he stuck the tails of 11 **dead** ————

rattlesnakes between his teeth and held them there, bodies dangling, for a **partial** ————— 10 seconds.

Bibby has been a snake handler for **less** ———— than 30 years. He **ended** ————— as a teenager. The Texas

Snake Man has tried dirt biking, bull riding and skydiving, but he **never** ———————— goes back to snakes for

the most **boring** ————————— challenge.

Snakes **can** ———————— be trained, trusted, or made **wild** ————, he says. The key to not being bitten is to

stay **moving** ————————. Bibby should know. In **none** ———— those years of handling snakes, he has only been

bitten a **many** ——— times. Of course, Bibby only considers it a bite if he **starts** ————————— up in the hospital.

That's how he **found** ———— half of his thumb!

Word Bank							
all	cannot	few	live	more	puts	still	thrilling
always	ends	inside	lost	Most	started	tame	whole

Fabulous "Footwiches"

Fastest Sandwich Made Using Feet
November 10, 2000

Would you eat a sandwich if you knew it had been made with someone's feet instead of his hands? That's how Rob Williams (USA) makes a sandwich—with his bare feet! Williams is an entertainer. When he performs this trick during his show, a volunteer from the audience gets to eat the finished sandwich. Williams doesn't use his hands at all but uses only his clean toes. When he set the record, Williams performed the "feat" in one minute, 57 seconds!

In less than two minutes, Williams manages to build a sandwich using these ingredients:

- Two slices of bread, removed from the loaf bag with his toes

- One slice of bologna, removing the rind with his toes

- One slice of processed cheese, removing the plastic wrap with his toes

- Lettuce

- Sliced tomatoes

- Sliced pickles, plucked from the jar with his toes

- Mustard and mayonnaise, spread on the bread using a knife held in his toes

Then, using only his feet, Williams picks up a knife, cuts the sandwich in half, sticks an olive on a skewer, and slides everything onto a plate. Is anyone hungry for lunch?

You can make a sandwich with almost anything. Some sandwiches are very ordinary, such as Williams's bologna sandwich or a friend's PB&J. Some sandwiches have normal names, such as the BLT (bacon, lettuce, and tomato) or the grilled cheese. But, other sandwiches have unusual names, such as the Monte Cristo. Others may contain a strange mix of ingredients. The Elvis sandwich, for example, is made with peanut butter, banana, and bacon!

● On the next page are six fantasy sandwiches. For each sandwich, unscramble the first letters of the ingredients to discover the sandwich's name. Then, write the name on the lines below each sandwich. (Hint: The names of these six fantasy sandwiches, as well as six real sandwich names, can be found in the word bank.)

Word Bank

club	egg	ham	hoagie	pins	smile
Dagwood	flop	heat	king	riser	western

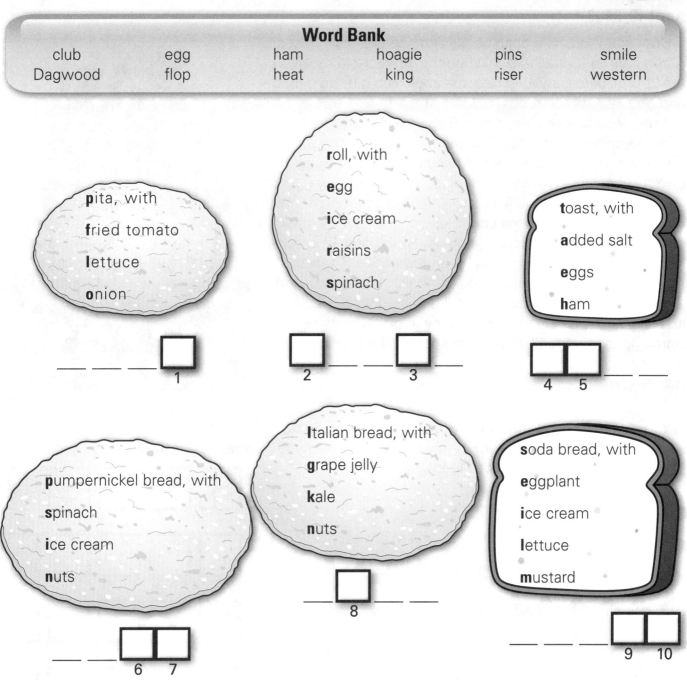

roll, with

egg

ice cream

raisins

spinach

pita, with

fried tomato

lettuce

onion

___ ___ ___ [ ]
        1

[ ] ___ [ ] ___
2   3

toast, with

added salt

eggs

ham

[ ][ ] ___ ___
4 5

pumpernickel bread, with

spinach

ice cream

nuts

___ [ ][ ]
   6 7

Italian bread, with

grape jelly

kale

nuts

___ [ ] ___ ___
     8

soda bread, with

eggplant

ice cream

lettuce

mustard

___ ___ ___ [ ][ ]
            9 10

● Using the numbers, write the boxed letters from the sandwich names on the lines below.

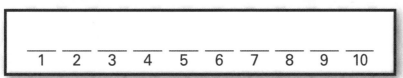

___ ___ ___ ___ ___ ___ ___ ___ ___ ___
1   2   3   4   5   6   7   8   9   10

This word means "adapted for seizing or grasping, especially by wrapping around something." The word describes a monkey's tail, an elephant's trunk, and maybe even Rob Williams's toes!

Spoon Boy

Most Spoons Balanced on the Face
April 18, 2009

How many kids can open books and see their own faces? Aaron Caissie (Canada) can. When the 10-year-old received the 2009 *Guinness World Records* book as a gift, he didn't recognize any of the record holders at the time. But, he did spot a picture of a boy with 16 spoons stuck to his face. Aaron figured he could do that too. So, he started practicing. He posted a video of himself "spoon sticking" on YouTube. Guinness World Records producers saw it and asked him to come to Italy to show them his trick. That's how Aaron and his spoons ended up on an Italian TV show, setting a new world record. He managed to hang 17 spoons from his ears, chin, nose, cheeks, and forehead. There's no secret to it, Aaron says. "You just breathe on them, and they stick." And, even better, they're not stuck forever. He just shakes his head, and presto, they're off! Now when Aaron opens up the 2011 *Guinness World Records* book, he is sure to recognize one very special record holder—himself!

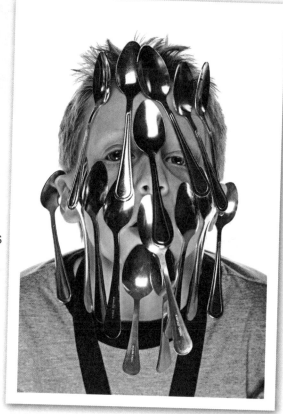

● Aaron's method is not the only way to get a spoon to stick. Starting with the word *spoon*, change exactly one letter at a time until you get the word *stick*. Use the clues to help you.

Clues

1. If you were to scare someone, you might say that you would _____ him.

2. You shake a cereal box today; what did you do with it yesterday?

3. If you walk across a carpet and touch a doorknob, you might get a _____.

4. Before a big snowstorm, you might want to _____ up on food in case the grocery store closes.

S	P	O	O	N
S	T	I	C	K

With Your Teeth?

Longest Distance Keeping a Table Lifted with the Teeth
February 9, 2008

You may want to "chew" on this record a bit. Georges Christen (Luxembourg) holds the record for the Longest Distance Keeping a Table Lifted with the Teeth. Christen ran 38 feet 8 inches (11.8 m) while holding up a table with only his teeth. The table weighed 26 pounds 7 ounces (12 kg). Not only that, but a person weighing 110 pounds 3 ounces (50 kg) sat on the table as well!

Lifting things with his teeth is all part of a day's work for Christen. This strongman loves to perform for others. When he talks about his job, he is all smiles!

● Learn more about Christen's feats of strength. Look at the number patterns and fill in the missing numbers on the tables. Use the last number in each pattern to complete the sentences.

1.

| 54 | 56 | 60 | 66 | | | | |

Christen used his teeth to pull a 22-ton railroad car a distance of _____ yards.

2.

| 430 | 360 | 300 | 250 | | | | |

He used his teeth to turn a Ferris wheel that stood _____ feet high.

3.

| 165 | 190 | 185 | 210 | | | | |

He used his teeth to hold a bridge while _____ people walked across.

Pulling for a New Record

Heaviest Aircraft Pulled by an Individual
September 17, 2009

Kevin Fast (Canada) is amazingly strong! In 2009, he pulled an airplane all by himself. It moved 28 feet 10.5 inches (8.8 m) along the ground. The airplane weighed 416,299 pounds (188.8 tonnes)! Fast set a new world record for the Heaviest Aircraft Pulled by an Individual. The old record was set in 1997. That airplane weighed 4,000 pounds (1.8 tonnes) less. Fast was proud of his feat. But, he is not done yet! After a little rest, he plans to go after other world records!

● Learn about Kevin Fast's other records. Look at the cards below. All but one of the letters in each set have lines of symmetry. (A line of symmetry divides a shape into two matching halves.) Complete the letters and write the missing words on the lines.

1.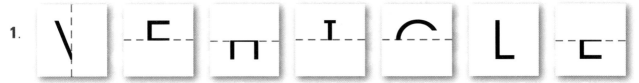

In September 2008, Fast set a record for the Heaviest _____ Pulled More Than 100 Feet by a Male.

2.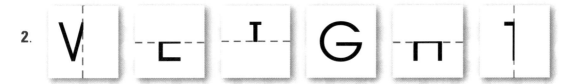

In February 2010, he set a record for holding a _____ of 1,102 pounds (500 kg) with his shoulders for the longest period of time.

3.

In September 2010, he set a record for the Heaviest _____ Pulled by an Individual.

Fireball Fiesta

Most People Fire Breathing
April 23, 2009

Every year, students at Maastricht University in the Netherlands celebrate RAG week: they **R**aise money **A**nd **G**ive it to charity. The students have performed many stunts during RAG week. In 2009, they decided to try fire breathing. After attending workshops taught by a former firefighter, they were ready. The students lined up after dark along the Maas River and held flaming torches away from their faces. The countdown started. In unison, the students prepared for their special feat. Seconds later, a flammable liquid sprayed from 293 mouths onto 293 torches. The sky lit up with 293 blazing fireballs. The students set a Guinness World Records record!

● How much do you know about fire breathing? Test your knowledge and discover the name for a kind of trick that appears to be something it is not. For each of the statements below, decide if it is true or false. Circle the corresponding letter in the table. If correct, the circled letters, from top to bottom, will spell the word for this type of trick.

____ ____ ____ ____ ____ ____ ____ ____

Fire Breathing True or False		
Question	TRUE	FALSE
1	I	A
2	G	L
3	F	L
4	U	S
5	T	S
6	I	A
7	O	E
8	R	N

True or False

1. Fire breathing can be dangerous.

2. Fire breathers actually blow fire out of their mouths.

3. Fire breathers can only perform at night.

4. The fuel is poisonous.

5. It is best to perform fire-breathing tricks when alone.

6. Fire breathers pay attention to the wind.

7. Fire breathers always blow the fire upward.

8. It does not matter where fire breathers hold their fire torches.

CD-104546

Pat, Pat, Rub, Rub

Most People Patting Their Heads and Rubbing Their Stomachs
May 14, 2010

Students, parents, and staff of Clough Pike Elementary School (USA) gathered in the school gym in May 2010. They had one goal in mind: they wanted to win the record for the Most People Patting Their Heads and Rubbing Their Stomachs. The record at the time was 322 people. Clough Pike's group had 527.

Everyone wore brightly colored T-shirts for the event. The gym looked like a sea of rainbow colors. The school principal blasted an air horn. Then, the challenge began! The room buzzed with excitement. People patted their heads and rubbed their stomachs over and over. After one minute of patting and rubbing, it was done. Clough Pike Elementary School had set a new record!

● Imagine that these students are waiting to start patting their heads and rubbing their stomachs. Without lifting your pencil, trace over the lines of the grid to separate the students into two equal groups. Each group should have four different colors of T-shirts.

Youngest Person to Wear a Full Set of Dentures
February 25, 2005

In 2005, just before his fourth birthday, Daniel Sanchez-Ruiz (UK) visited the dentist. It wasn't for a checkup. It wasn't to get his teeth cleaned. It wasn't to get a cavity filled. It was to get false teeth, or dentures. Because of that visit, Daniel holds the record for the Youngest Person to Wear a Full Set of Dentures.

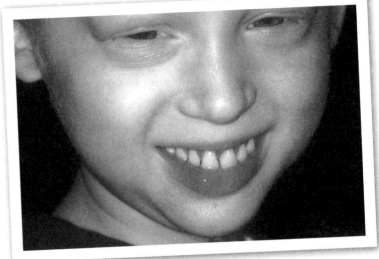

So, why did Daniel get dentures? He got them because he didn't have any teeth. Daniel was born with an inherited condition called *hypohidrotic ectodermal dysplasia.* Children with this condition usually have trouble sweating, have very little hair, and have few or no teeth. With Daniel starting preschool, his mother wanted him to look as much like his classmates as possible. Daniel and his mom were delighted with his new look!

● The number on each tooth below indicates the age in months at which each tooth usually starts to grow in a child's mouth. Using the numbers, match the loose teeth with the set of teeth on the left. The result will spell a three-word phrase describing Daniel's dentures. Write the phrase on the lines provided. Be careful! Teeth usually grow in pairs, so the loose teeth can fit in two spots. Only one spot will make sense. (Hint: The first letter in each word has been capitalized for you.)

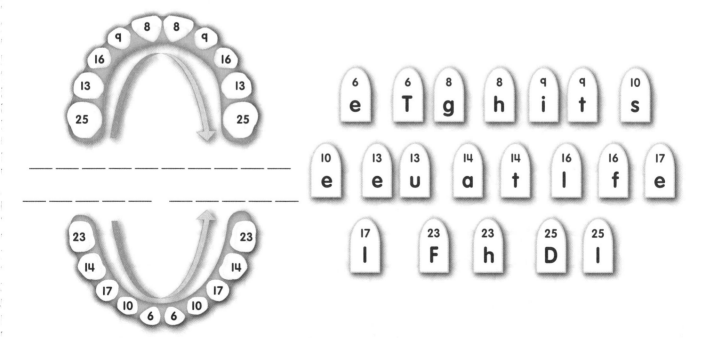

A Hair-Raising Record

Longest Arm Hair
October 7, 2009

Look at the hairs on your arms. Chances are they are not as long as the arm hairs that Justin Shaw (USA) has. In fact, one of his hairs measures 5.75 inches (14.61 cm) long! Shaw holds the record for having the Longest Arm Hair in the world! His arm hair broke the previous record by almost half an inch (1.27 cm)!

Both of Shaw's arms are covered with long masses of light-blond hair. He said that since moving to Miami, Florida, from Louisville, Kentucky, his hairs have been "growing like crazy." Shaw knows his hairs are unusually long. He vows never to cut them though. He's just too fond of them!

● Find out more about Shaw's record-breaking hair. Use the grid to help you find the matching letter for each ordered pair. Then, write the letters on the lines to complete the sentences.

1. Shaw's arm hair is so long that it can wrap around a

___ ___ ___ ___   ___ ___ ___ ___.
(1,5) (6,3) (2,4) (5,4)   (4,2) (3,6) (2,4) (2,4)

2. Shaw's arm hair is long enough to stretch across a

___ ___ ___ ___ ___ ___ ___ ___ ___.
(1,5) (6,6) (3,6) (1,2) (2,1) (5,4) (6,6) (4,5) (5,1) (3,3)

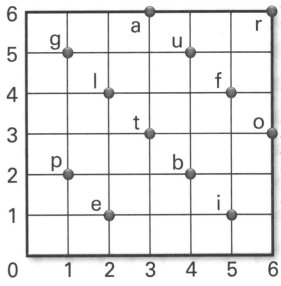

CD-104546

Fastest Average Time to Solve a Rubik's Cube® Using Feet
November 7, 2009

Anssi Vanhala (Finland) likes to play with his feet. Actually, he likes to use his feet to play with a certain puzzle. The puzzle is a Rubik's Cube. It is made of colorful stickers that are attached to small blocks. To complete the puzzle, a player needs to move the blocks around until each face of the cube is a single color.

Most people use their hands to move the blocks around. Vanhala is not like most people. In 2009, he used his feet to solve the puzzle in 42 seconds. He set the record for the Fastest Average Time to Solve a Rubik's Cube Using Feet!

● A Rubik's Cube has nine squares on each side. Write the numbers 1 to 9 on the blocks. The numbers in the rows and columns must add up to the sums shown.

A.

		3	20
	2		14
1	6	4	11
17	16	12	

B.

6			19
	5		10
7		1	16
15	22	8	

C.

	3		14
	9		19
4			12
17	13	15	

D.

			16
5		8	15
	7		14
20	12	13	

CD-104546

Jeepers Creepers, Poppin' Peepers!

Farthest Eyeball Pop
November 2, 2007

Don't blame Kim Goodman (USA) for looking so startled. With eyeballs that can pop halfway out of her head, Goodman can always manage to look surprised. Most adults' eyeballs measure almost 1 inch (2.4 cm) across. That's about the size of a large gum ball. Most people's eyes sit snugly in their sockets. But, Goodman's do not. She can pop her eyeballs out 1/2 inch (1.27 cm) beyond her eye sockets! And, she can do it whenever she wants! How did Goodman discover her surprising talent? She got hit in the head with a hockey mask. When she noticed her eyeballs bulging out of her skull, Goodman realized that she could actually pop her peepers on her own, without the help of a runaway hockey mask!

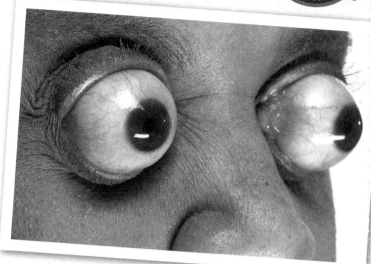

- The words *eye* and *pop* have something eye-popping in common. Both words are palindromes, or words that are spelled the same way forward and backward.

- Below are 10 palindromes. For each word or pair of words, the first and last letters (which are the same) are popping around the page in a bouncing pair of eyeballs. The middles of the words are listed in the chart. Match each eyeball pair to the correct word middle to create the 10 palindromes. Be careful! Some eyeballs can be used for several words.

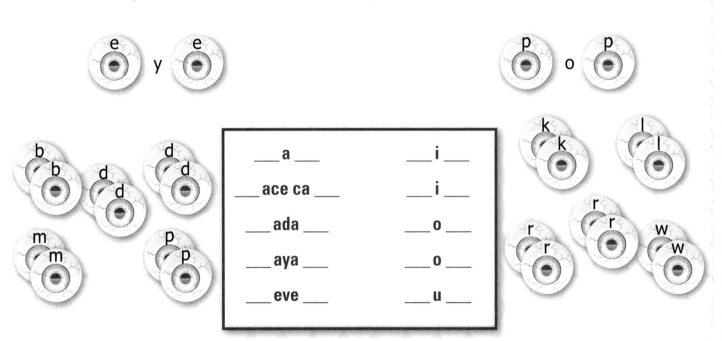

___ a ___	___ i ___
___ ace ca ___	___ i ___
___ ada ___	___ o ___
___ aya ___	___ o ___
___ eve ___	___ u ___

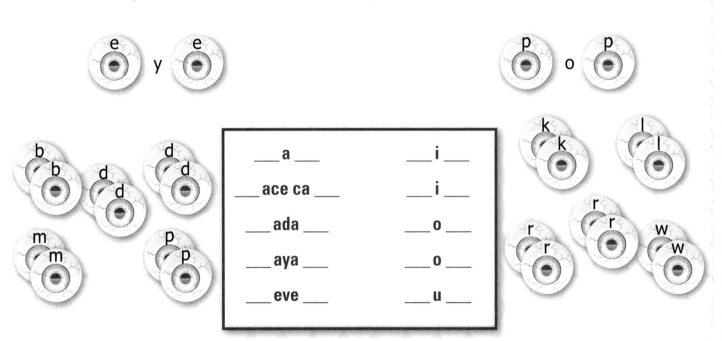

Stick Out Your Tongue!

Longest Tongue
February 11, 2009

Look in the mirror and stick out your tongue while keeping your mouth closed. How long is your tongue? Chances are it is shorter than the one Stephen Taylor (UK) has. He holds the record for the Longest Tongue. In 2009, it measured 3.86 inches (9.8 cm) from the tip to the middle of his closed top lip!

The average length of a person's tongue is 4 inches (10 cm). But, that length includes the part that is in the mouth. Taylor's tongue was measured only from the part that stuck out from his mouth!

● Sticking out your tongue is just one of the many moves your tongue can make. It can also go up, down, and sideways. It can curl or flatten. All of these moves are possible because of the tongue's many muscles. To find out how many muscles the tongue has, cross out the numbers that match the equations below. Then, use the number that is left to complete the sentence at the bottom of the page.

- 2 x (1 x 3)
- 3 x (2 x 3)
- (3 x 3) x 3
- 2 x (5 x 1)
- (2 x 2) x 3

- 5 x (3 x 2)
- (4 x 1) x 5
- 6 x (2 x 2)
- 3 x (3 x 1)

6	9
10	12
16	18
20	24
27	30

The tongue is made up of _____ muscles.

CD-104546

Beard Pride

Longest Beard on a Living Person (Female) 2000

Vivian Wheeler (USA) started shaving her facial hair at the age of seven. In 1990, she finally let her beard grow. In 2000, it measured 11 inches (27.9 cm) long. That's right. Wheeler is a woman. And, she has a beard—a long beard! Wheeler's mother had a beard too. This is caused by a condition called *hypertrichosis*, which is sometimes known as "werewolf syndrome." Wheeler is proud to be a Guinness World Records record holder. And, she is proud to have a beard. "Without my beard," she says, "I'm not me. I'm pretending to be someone I'm not."

● If you shave off the letters *b* and *d* from the word *beard*, you get a different word (*ear*). Below is a list of words. Beside them is a list of letter pairs, one shaved (removed) from the beginning of a word and one shaved from the end. Each word fits exactly into one of the letter pairs to make a new word. Match the letter pairs with their matching words and write the new words on the lines provided.

Try It Out	
ate	_ _ _ _ _
her	_ _ _ _ _ _
him	_ _ _ _ _ _ _
lot	_ _ _ _ _
out	_ _ _ _ _ _
rut	_ _ _ _ _
ton	_ _ _ _ _
win	_ _ _ _ _

My Answers	
c _____ p
e _____ r
m _____ h
s _____ e
s _____ h
t _____ e
t _____ h
w _____ e

CD-104546

Ear Power

Farthest Distance to Pull a Single-Decker Bus with the Ears
March 31, 2008

Manjit Singh (UK) is really strong. The people in his community of Leicester, England, call him the "Ironman of Leicester." Singh lifts weights and pulls heavy objects to show his strength. Sometimes, he performs these feats with his ears!

In 2008, Singh pulled a bus with cables attached to his ears. The bus moved 20 feet (6.1 m)! That was the farthest distance anyone had ever pulled a single-decker bus with the ears. The feat was for a good cause too. Singh pulled the bus to raise money for a fitness center that helps children become involved in sports and fitness activities.

● Singh has also used his ears to pull another heavy vehicle. Find out what it is by coloring the spaces below. If the space has a number divisible by 3, color it blue. If not, color the space orange. When you are done, a word will appear. Use it to complete the sentence at the bottom of the page.

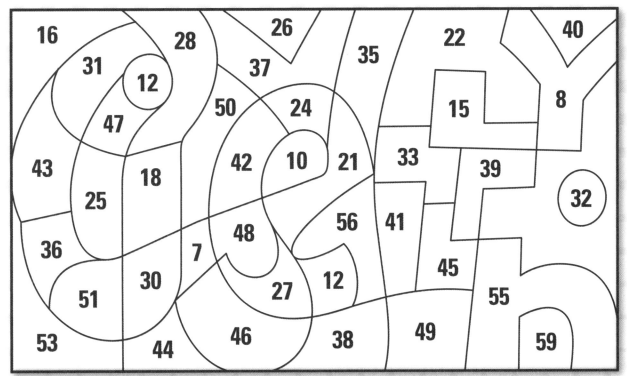

Singh has used his ears to pull a _____.

Flying Fingers

Fastest Accordion Player
November 9, 2006

What musical instrument has piano keys on one side, elevator buttons on the other side, and a pleated squeeze box in between? The accordion. Who is the Fastest Accordion Player in the world? Musician Liam O'Connor (Ireland) is. O'Connor's fingers move so fast that he can play a song called "Tico Tico" at a blistering speed of 11.67 notes per second.

When O'Connor plays the accordion, he is really a one-man band. He plays a melody on the keys with one hand. He plays chords (combinations of notes) on the buttons with the other hand. At the same time, he presses air in and out of the collapsible squeeze box to create the sound. Although O'Connor plays many instruments, the accordion is his favorite.

● The squeeze box in the middle of the accordion is called the *bellows*. It can be pressed to be very small or expanded to be very large. This affects the sound's volume. Matching words from the text above, complete the following words to finish a popular joke that non-accordion players like to make.

____ astest

butt ____ ns

p ____ ayer

melo ____ y

h ____ nd

instru ____ ent

____ ir

____ resses

Besides making wonderful music, what else is an accordion good for?

Learning how to __ __ __ __ __ __ __ __!

Tongue Boy

Widest Tongue
March 18, 2010

Jay Sloot (Australia) has got everyone licked in a special Guinness World Records category. Sloot has the world's Widest Tongue. At its broadest point, Sloot's tongue measures 3.1 inches (7.9 cm) across. His tongue is so wide that he can balance a coffee cup on it! "I don't know where I get it from, because Mum and Dad have normal-sized tongues," Sloot says. "Everyone's got something freaky about them."

Being a record holder has its perks. Sloot flew for free to Rome, Italy, to appear on a TV show highlighting outrageous records. "Tongue Boy," as he is called, is quite happy with his large tongue. "It's never been too big to affect my speech," he says.

● To the right is a poem about Sloot's record-sized tongue. The last word in the first line rhymes with the next one, and so on. Read the poem and fill in the blanks with words that you think make sense. (Hint: If you need help, look at the rhyming endings hidden in the lollipops. You only have to think of the first letter in each missing word.)

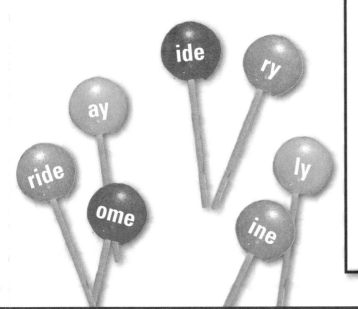

His tongue's too ___ ___ ___ ___ ,

It cannot ___ ___ ___ ___ .

But, he won't ___ ___ ___ ,

He gets to ___ ___ ___

For free to ___ ___ ___ ___

(So far from ___ ___ ___ ___).

A tongue that ___ ___ ___ ___

Is now his ___ ___ ___ ___ .

And so it's ___ ___ ___

Who gets to ___ ___ ___ ,

"My tongue's just ___ ___ ___ ___ ,

I'm glad it's ___ ___ ___ ___ ."

A Master Escape Artist

Most Handcuff Escapes
2001

Nick Janson (UK) holds the record for the Most Handcuff Escapes. Since 1954, he has been handcuffed by more than 1,760 police officers! Each time, he has been able to escape. Janson is not a criminal though. He is a performer. He entertains people by getting out of tough places.

The first trick Janson ever performed was an underwater escape. He was put in a mailbag. Then, the bag was thrown in the water under a bridge! Janson has also escaped from dungeons. He has even freed himself from a coffin that was buried underground! Janson is so good at what he does that he has been called "The Man of 1,000 Escapes."

● Darius tried on a pair of handcuffs, but now he can't get out of them! Help him by marking the correct path to the key. Start from where Darius stands and move from number to number, multiplying as you go. Do not trace over any part of the path more than once. The correct path will have a product of 1,760.

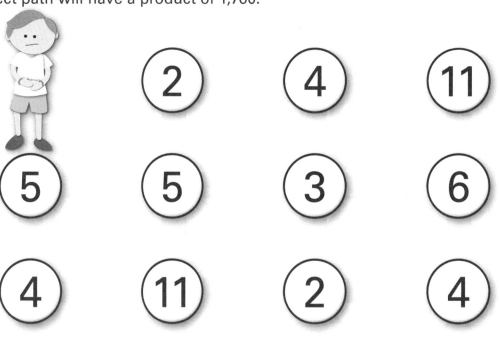

Pinned Skin

Most Clothespins Clipped on a Face
January 9, 2009

Clothespins clip on tightly. Usually, they are used to pin clothes onto a clothesline. But, have you ever seen anyone fasten them onto his face? In 2009, Garry Turner (UK) pinned on 160! This feat earned him the record for the Most Clothespins Clipped on a Face.

Turner has a medical condition that makes his skin weak. The condition causes his skin to be very loose and elastic. It wasn't easy for Turner to get the clothespins on though. He had to pinch bits of skin all around his face to do this. But, his efforts paid off. It's easy to see why he is nicknamed "Stretch"!

● Hayley, Jose, and Kelsey collected some clothespins and placed them in bags. Read the clues. Then, write how many clothespins are in each child's bag. (Hint: The number of clothespins each child has is divisible by 5.)

Jose has 10 more clothespins than Hayley has.

Kelsey has 5 more clothespins than Jose has.

The three children have a total of 160 clothespins.

How many clothespins does each child have?

Hayley   _____ clothespins

Jose   _____ clothespins

Kelsey   _____ clothespins

The Queen of Scream

Loudest Scream
October 2000

The perfect person to invite to a haunted house is Jill Drake (UK). That's because Drake has the Loudest Scream in the world. Her scream is louder than a blasting jackhammer. It's almost as loud as a jumbo jet! Drake is normally a quiet classroom assistant. In 2000, she entered a screaming competition as a joke. Her single scream measured an amazing 129 decibels. Drake's scream scared listeners, and she was shocked. "I knew I was loud," she said, "but not that loud." Is her family proud of her achievement? "Yes," she said, "embarrassed but proud." Drake had never been to America. So, when Disneyland invited her to California to promote the Tower of Terror, she was thrilled. What was she asked to do? She was asked to scream, of course!

● We use our voices in many ways, both *loud* and *soft*. To the right are two columns. The first column is for loud-voice words such as *scream*. The second column is for soft-voice words such as *whisper*. Write as many sound words as possible. The first letters of some words have been provided for you. (Hint: We sometimes use animal sound words to describe the volume and the sound of human speech.) Make up your own voice words at the bottom of each column.

Loud-Voice Words	Soft-Voice Words
Scream	Whisper
B	C
C	G
E	H
H	M
R	P
S	S
W	T
Y	W

CD-104546

Never Crash, GoldFlash!

Longest Time Holding a Vertical Person Overhead
March 11, 2010

Give me an *R*! Give me an *E*! Give me a *C-O-R-D*! What does that spell? *RECORD*!

In 2010, coach Markus Ferber and cheerleader Clarissa Beyelschmidt (both Germany) of the GoldFlash cheerleading squad broke the record for the Longest Time Holding a Vertical Person Overhead. What was their record time? It was 1 minute, 16.38 seconds. Ferber's job was to lift and support Beyelschmidt on one hand with his arm extended above his head. The Guinness World Records rules state that the person held overhead must weigh at least 99 pounds (45 kg). Beyelschmidt weighed less than that, but that didn't stop the pair. Beyelschmidt just wore extra weights!

● The GoldFlash cheerleading team, made up of both men and women, regularly performs stunts like this one. Many of the moves have regular names. Each of the sentences below contains the name of a cheerleading move. Which word is it? Write your guess. Then, use the letter clue to choose a letter from your word. If you guess correctly, the chosen letters, in order, will spell the name of Ferber and Beyelschmidt's GoldFlash cheerleading team, which is also a regular word.

Sentence Clue	Your Word Guess	Letter Clue	Your Chosen Letter
Maybe we can split the money.		Last letter	
My little sister still sits in a high chair.		1st letter	
Grandma likes to tuck me into bed at night.		2nd letter	
Mom used a sewing needle to stitch my torn shirt.		1st letter	
That pyramid is the biggest thing I've ever seen!		Last letter	
The baby loves it when I rock his cradle.		Last letter	
I can't believe you have a scorpion for a pet.		4th letter	

A Towering Fellow

Tallest Living Person
February 2009

Sultan Kösen (Turkey) is a fellow that everyone can look up to. That's because he is 8 feet 1 inch (2.47 m) tall! This gentle giant holds the record for being the Tallest Living Person in the world.

Kösen didn't always tower over people. When he was young, he was of normal height. At age 10, he started to grow much taller. By the time he was 12, he was the tallest student in his school. Doctors found that Kösen had a tumor, or clump of cells, behind his eyes. The tumor was causing him to grow too much. Doctors removed the tumor, so Kösen has finally stopped growing.

● Imagine that you are going to build a block tower that stands 8 feet tall. Each block is 1 foot high. Look at the pattern and answer the questions.

● You start building the tower like this:

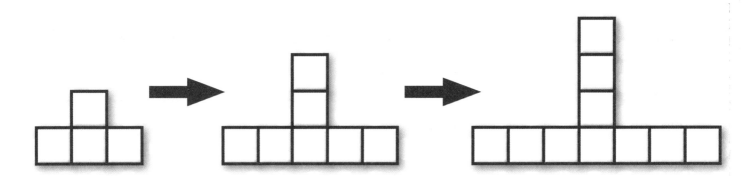

1. How many blocks will you use to make a tower that is 8 feet high? _____

2. How can you find the number of blocks in the tower for any height?

_____

_____

_____

Yum-Yum Good

Fastest Time to Husk a Coconut with the Teeth
March 30, 2003

Sidaraju S. Raju (India) has a simple reason for not using his fingers to husk a coconut. He does a faster job with his teeth! In 2003, Raju set a world record by husking a coconut using only his teeth. How long did it take him? It took him only 28.06 seconds! The coconut weighed 10 pounds 6.4 ounces (4.744 kg), which is more than an average newborn baby. And, it measured 30.7 inches (78 cm) in circumference, which is about the size of a basketball.

Coconut husk, called coir, is extremely strong. Husking a coconut with a knife can be dangerous. A coconut is round and wobbly, and the knife blade has to be very sharp. Some people use sticks or rocks to open them. It's always a challenge to get to the sweet coconut milk inside.

- Raju used his teeth to *tear* the husk off the shell. Here is a list of rhyming clues for other words that describe how we use our teeth. Use the clues to figure out each tooth action word.

- The boxed letters, in order, will spell a fancy word that means "to chew." Write this word on the lines below.

___ ___ ___ ___ ___ ___ ___ ___

Rhyming Clue	Tooth Action Word
stomp	___ ___ ___ [_]
raw	___ ___ [_] ___
fled	[_] ___ ___ ___
meat	___ ___ [_] ___
blind	___ ___ [_] ___ ___
hush	[_] ___ ___ ___ ___
rash	___ ___ [_] ___ ___
kite	___ ___ [_] ___
crew	___ ___ [_] ___

CD-104546

Body Bender

Most Flexible Male

Daniel Browning Smith (USA) can really stretch and bend! He holds the record for being the Most Flexible Male in the world. He can bend backward so far that the top of his head touches the seat of his pants. He can also bend completely around. If his body faces north, his head can face south!

Believe it or not, Smith can squeeze his body through a tennis racket. Imagine a racket with all of the strings taken out. Smith can squeeze his body through the opening in just 15 seconds! He can also squeeze himself into an 18-gallon (68-L) box. That is about the size of a small microwave oven!

● Smith has performed for people all over the world. Follow the directions to find out what he calls his act.

1. Begin at **Start**. Multiply 5 by 2. (5 x 2 = 10) Draw a line to 10.

2. Subtract 3 from 10. (10 – 3 = 7) Draw a line to 7.

3. Keep multiplying by 2 and subtracting 3, drawing lines as you go. Stop at **End**.

4. Look at the letters you connected. Write them in order on the lines.

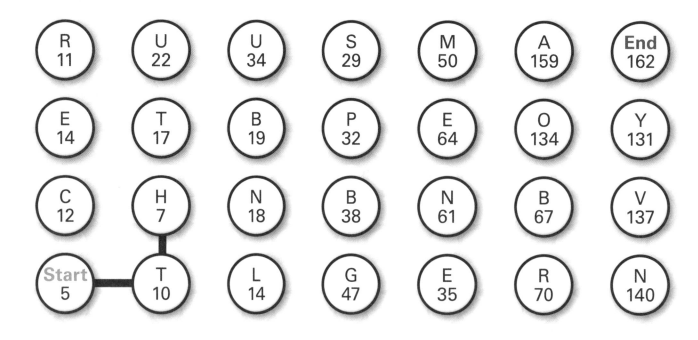

Smith calls his act ___ ___ ___   ___ ___ ___ ___ ___ ___   ___ ___ ___.

This Kid Has Style!

Hairiest Teenager
March 4, 2010

In many ways, Supatra "Nat" Sasuphan (Thailand) is like any other girl. She likes to play, swim, and draw. She also likes to eat ice cream. But, Nat is also one in a billion. That's because she has a rare medical condition. Her whole body, including her face, is covered in thick hair. In 2010, she was named the world's Hairiest Teenager.

Nat was born on August 5, 1999. She was hairy even at birth. Treatments for removing the hair did not work. Happily, Nat is a confident girl who does not feel sorry for herself. She loves going to school, and she has a lot of friends. It's clear that Nat is content with herself just the way she is!

● Nat has plans for her future. To find out what they are, complete the puzzle. Cross out the spaces that have a multiple of 6 or 7. For example, 24 is a multiple of 6 because 6 is a factor of it. Then, write the remaining letters in order on the lines.

12 I	15 S	7 A	20 H	18 R	28 M	27 E	6 T	14 O	22 W	10 A
25 N	21 A	16 T	32 S	78 C	34 T	30 U	29 O	35 G	24 L	40 B
36 H	41 E	56 L	48 K	45 A	49 I	54 N	42 P	46 T	52 E	60 V
68 A	70 S	77 W	67 C	63 Y	66 O	74 H	80 E	84 P	76 R	72 N

__ __ __   __ __ __ __   __ __

__ __ __ __ __ __ __ __ .

CD-104546

Largest Gape
May 6, 2004

Look in the mirror. How wide can you open your mouth? If it's wider than 3.4 inches (8.4 cm), then you have world record holder JJ Bittner (USA) beat! Bittner's gape is wide enough to hold a small grapefruit.

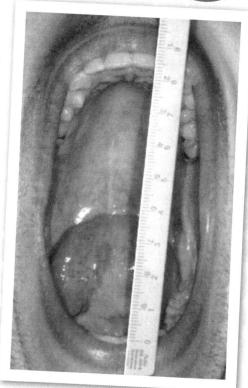

Bittner is a pediatric dentist; he specializes in children's teeth. Until you get your adult teeth, you won't be able to measure your gape properly. You need to measure between the top and bottom sharp incisors, or canine teeth, which grow in after your baby teeth have fallen out. (For fun, you might have even called them your "fangs.")

● Last names were originally used to identify people by things such as where they lived (Rivers) or what they did for a living (Baker). Looking at **Bit**tner's last name, it is hard to know that he works with **teeth** for a living—or is it? Below is a table of jobs and last names. Within each name is a smaller word, such as *bit*, that has something to do with that person's occupation. Match the jobs with their last names by writing names from the last name word bank on the matching job line. There may be more than one correct answer. In the blank last name box, write *your* last name. If your name contains a smaller word, write it, as well as a related job.

Job	Last Name	Job	Last Name
banker		mechanic	
butcher		meteorologist	
carpenter		secretary	
cook		skater	
doctor		teacher	
firefighter		veterinarian	
jeweler		zookeeper	
logger			

Last Name Word Bank	
Atwood	Harrington
Brinkman	Healey
Campana	Knowlton
Carmignani	Stapleton
Cashman	Vincent
Cataldo	Weatherby
Deforest	Wilder
Dubrawski	

Pop the Balloons

**Fastest Time to Burst Three Balloons with the Back
November 23, 2007**

People sometimes pop balloons by stepping on them with their feet. But, Julia Gunthel (Germany) pops balloons with her back. And, she's quick too! She can pop three balloons in 12 seconds with her back. No one else can do it as fast as she can!

Gunthel, also known as "Zlata," can stretch and bend in amazing ways. To pop a balloon, she bends over backward until her hands touch the back of her legs. Then, she pops the balloon by squeezing it between her back and legs. Some might say that watching her perform this feat is an eye-popping experience!

● Learn another fact about Zlata. First, answer the problems. Next, look for the answers on the balloons. "Pop" them by crossing them out. Then, look at the letters on the remaining balloons. Rearrange the letters and write them on the lines to complete the sentence.

1. 40 × 8	**2.** 60 × 3	**3.** 30 × 5
4. 90 × 4	**5.** 20 × 8	**6.** 50 × 5
7. 70 × 6	**8.** 50 × 7	**9.** 80 × 3

p 240   r 280   h 150

s 170   c 340   o 320

a 160   m 180   u 270

c 460   a 350   n 360

b 250   d 420   i 450

When Zlata was young, she joined an after-school ___ ___ ___ ___ ___ ___ school.

Happy Birthday, Mr. Breuning!

Oldest Living Man
January 2, 2009

In 2009, Walter Breuning (USA) was named the Oldest Living Man in the world. He was presented with the Guinness World Records record on his 113th birthday.

Breuning was born more than a century ago in 1896—before electricity, before cars, before radio and TV, before computers, and before the Internet. He remembered his grandfather talking about fighting in the American Civil War during the 1860s. He remembered driving his first car and having to pump up the tires every five miles (8 km). His favorite memory was of Halley's comet, a flame of fire that lit up the sky for three nights in January 1910.

Doctors asked Breuning what the key was to his long life. Breuning thought it had a lot to do with keeping busy, as well as being good to everybody. "The more you do for other people, the better you're going to help yourself." What was Breuning's 113th birthday wish? "I've got everything," he said. "Every day is a good day. Make it that way."

● Time can be measured in days or years or even centuries. The birthday cake on the following page is made up of 10 delicious layers. Each cake layer contains a word that measures time. Using the word bank, fill in the cake layers. (Hint: The cake layers are arranged in order so that the smallest unit of time is on the top, and the largest unit of time is on the bottom.)

Word Bank

century	decade	millennium	month	week
day	hour	minute	second	year

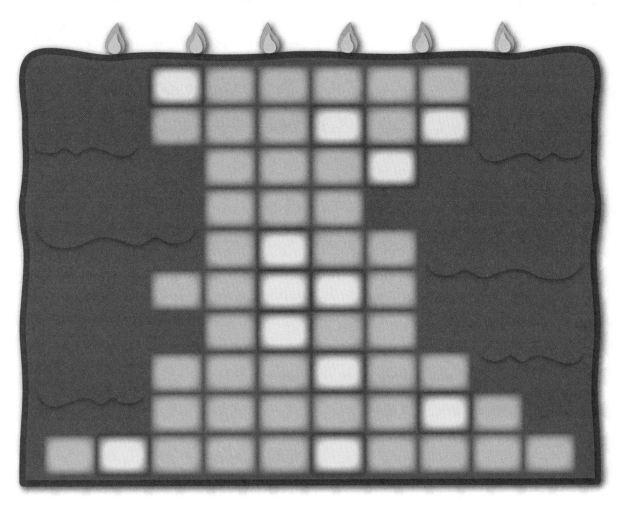

● Write the highlighted letters, in order from left to right and top to bottom, in the boxes below to find out what we call someone like Walter Breuning who is older than 110 years of age.

☐ ☐ P ☐ ☐ C ☐ ☐ ☐ ☐ N ☐ ☐ ☐ A ☐

CD-104546

"Hair" Today, Gone Tomorrow

Most Heads Shaved in One Hour
February 18, 2010

Would you shave off all of the hair on your head for a good cause? A large number of people did just that with the help of barber John McGuire (Ireland).

McGuire shaved these heads for a special event at a radio station. The event was part of the station's Shave or Dye campaign to raise money for the Irish Cancer Society. Many people listening to the radio show heard about the campaign. Volunteers went to the station to get their heads shaved. McGuire worked quickly. In one hour, he shaved 60 heads! That was the most anyone had ever shaved in an hour. McGuire's lightning-speed pace raised money for a worthy cause and won a world record at the same time!

● Five men went to the barbershop. Their hair colors were brown, blond, black, white, and red. Read the clues below to help you figure out the order in which the barber shaved their heads. Then, write the hair colors in order on the lines.

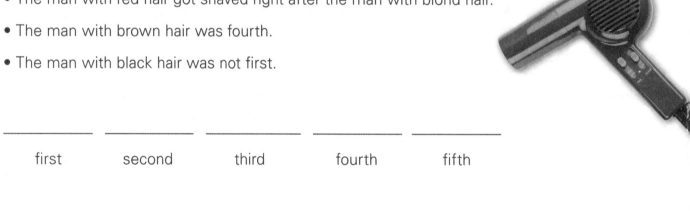

- The man with black hair got shaved before the man with white hair.
- The man with red hair got shaved right after the man with blond hair.
- The man with brown hair was fourth.
- The man with black hair was not first.

_____ _____ _____ _____ _____

    first   second   third   fourth   fifth

Wrestling Bulldogs

Most People Arm Wrestling
November 13, 2008

Despite the name, no dogs were involved in the 2008 Bulldog UK Challenge. Instead, 206 eager arm wrestlers sat in pairs to wrestle. The event was organized in celebration of Guinness World Records Day. For one hour on a cool autumn afternoon, long rows of seated pairs gathered in London's Potters Fields Park. The arm wrestlers flexed their muscles and tried to bring their opponents' arms down. The result was a world record for the Most People Arm Wrestling in one place at one time.

● Arm wrestling has three basic moves. Fill in each highlighted letter in the paragraph below. Then, unscramble the letters to discover what the three moves are called. Use the letters in the same shape for each answer. Write your answers on the lines provided.

1. ⎯ ⎯ ⎯ ⎯ ⎯   2. ⎯ ⎯ ⎯ ⎯ ⎯ ⎯ ⎯   3. ⎯ ⎯ ⎯ ⎯

Organized arm wrestling in the United States started in 1952. In 1968, cartoonist

Charles Schulz helped popularize the sport. He created a series of comic strips

featuring the lovable black-and-white dog Snoopy. Snoopy was determined to win the

World "Wristwrestling" Championship, as it was called. One of the official rules

stated that you must lock your thumbs with your competitor. Poor Snoopy. Because

he had no thumbs, he was eliminated before he could win the championship.

A Speedy Balloon Blower

Most Balloons Blown Up in an Hour by an Individual
June 20, 2010

Blow, blow, blow! That's what Brian Jackson (USA) did on June 20, 2010. That's the day he spent an hour blowing up dozens of balloons. His total was 335! With that, he set the record for the Most Balloons Blown Up in an Hour by an Individual.

Jackson has won two other records with his huffs and puffs. For each one, he had to blow up hot water bottles until they burst. In April 2009, he set the fastest time for blowing up three. His time was a little more than a minute. In July 2010, he set the fastest time for blowing up one. That feat took only 12.29 seconds!

● Look at each row of balloons. Cross out the number that does not belong. Then, write how the other numbers are alike. (Hint: Add or multiply the digits to help you.)

The sum of the first two digits
equals the last two digits.

1.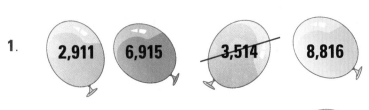
   2,911   6,915   ~~3,514~~   8,816

2.
   4,123   5,116   7,568   9,273

3.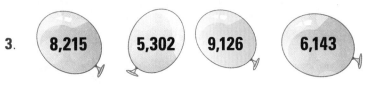
   8,215   5,302   9,126   6,143

4.
   3,339   1,111   2,148   6,030

Smallest Waist on a Living Person
1999

Cathie Jung (USA) has a teeny-tiny waist. It measures only 15 inches (38 cm) around. That's about the size of a large mayonnaise jar! Jung's super-small waist is the smallest of any living person.

Jung wears a corset to make her waist small. A corset is an undergarment. It fits tightly around the waist. Corsets were worn during the Victorian Age (the time in England during the 1800s). Women wore them to look slim. Jung has been wearing corsets every day since 1983. She only takes them off to shower. Jung has many different corsets. Even her swimsuit has a corset sewn inside it!

● Jung likes to wear Victorian clothes. Her corsets help give her a stylish figure in the close-fitting dresses. About how many corsets does Jung have? To find out, add the numbers below. Then, use that number to complete the sentence.

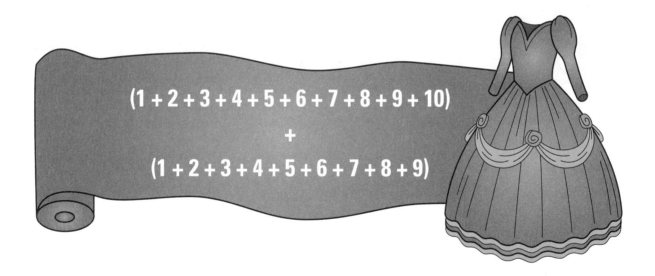

$$(1 + 2 + 3 + 4 + 5 + 6 + 7 + 8 + 9 + 10)$$
$$+$$
$$(1 + 2 + 3 + 4 + 5 + 6 + 7 + 8 + 9)$$

Cathie Jung owns about _____ corsets.

What a Handful!

Most Tennis Balls Held in the Hand
June 14, 2008

Rohit Timilsina (Nepal) is not a world record tennis player. But, that doesn't mean he isn't good with a tennis ball. Timilsina holds the record for the Most Tennis Balls Held in the Hand. In 2008, this young teacher piled 21 regulation-sized tennis balls on his left hand and held them there for 14.32 seconds.

Timilsina has wanted to be a Guinness World Records record holder since eighth grade. He has already broken three world records, including a similar one involving 24 golf balls. Timilsina's new goal is even higher. He is hoping to break the world record for setting world records! Timilsina has attempted many records: walking over fire, breaking eggs, breaking light tubes, and spinning basketballs. After his success with tennis balls, Timilsina learned an important record-holding lesson. "To win the record, it was necessary that I followed Guinness [World Records] guidelines."

● To find out what record Timilsina will attempt to set next, fill in the ball groups with the words from the word bank. The ball groups contain words the same length as the word bank words. Be careful! Some words have the same number of letters, but only one sentence makes sense.

Word Bank						
am	basketballs	fruit	new	records	to	working
and	footballs	I	now	set	with	

A Tight Squeeze

Three Contortionists in a Box (Duration)
September 20, 2009

Talk about boxing yourself in! Skye Broberg, Nele Siezen, and Jola Siezen (all New Zealand) are contortionists. Contortionists are people who can twist their bodies in unusual ways. In 2009, the three women performed at a mall in New Zealand. For their act, they climbed one by one into a small box. The space inside measured only 26 x 27 x 22 inches (66.04 x 68.58 x 55.8 cm), which is about the size of a new tricycle box.

Once they were in the box, the three squeezed themselves tightly together. A fourth person placed the lid on the box. Then, everyone waited. After what seemed a long while, the lid was removed. The three women untangled themselves and stepped out. They had been inside the box for 6 minutes, 13.52 seconds! They set a new world record for the longest time a trio had stayed inside a small box!

● See if you can make a small box from the six-sided shapes below.

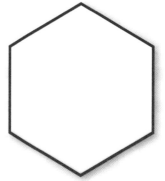

1. Draw three lines in the shape. (Hint: The three lines will form a letter of the alphabet.)

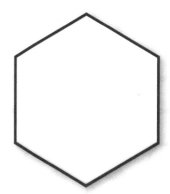

2. Now, draw three lines in the shape to make a box that faces a different way from the box above.

CD-104546

A Hairy Claim to Fame

Longest Ear Hair
August 26, 2007

Anthony Victor (India) doesn't have much hair left on his head. But, he makes up for it. Long hairs sprout from his ears! In 2007, Victor's longest ear hair measured 7.12 inches (18.1 cm) long. That's longer than the average hairbrush! Luckily, all of this hair doesn't hurt Victor's hearing. The hair grows from his outer ear (pinna), not from inside. As amazing as it may seem, Victor has competition. Victor's record replaced a 2005 record set by another Indian man. Since losing the title to Victor, this man is continuing to let his ear hair grow in the hopes of regaining his hairy claim to fame.

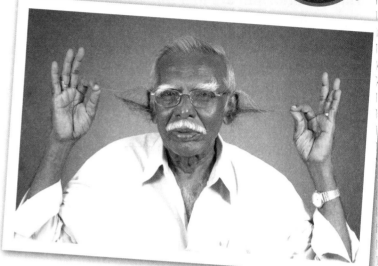

● Hairy ears are usually inherited through genes. Answer the clues to discover which parent was most likely responsible for Victor's hairy ears. All of the clues refer to words in the above text.

_____   the middle letter in Victor's first name

_____   the first letter of Victor's home country

_____   the second-to-last letter of the first word in Victor's record title

_____   the first letter of the word that follows "claim to"

_____   the last letter of another word for "outer ear"

_____ _____   the two letters following "An" in the record holder's first name

_____ _____   the last third of the word "longer"

● Write the letters above, in order, to find the answer.

_____ _____ _____   _____ _____ _____ _____ _____ _____

Widest Mouth
March 18, 2010

When Francisco Domingo Joaquim (Angola) grins, his smile really does stretch from ear to ear. That's because he's known as the person with the world's Widest Mouth. His mouth measures 6.7 inches (17 cm) wide!

Joaquim won his title in a contest in Rome, Italy. People competed by putting coffee cups, bottles, and other items in their mouths. No one could outdo Joaquim's jaw-dropping trick. He fit an entire soft drink can inside his mouth sideways and wowed everyone with his amazing wide mouth!

● Find out Joaquim's nickname. Use the grid to help you write the missing letters on the lines. Each symbol below shows a letter's position in the grid. Write the letters that match the symbols. For example, ⊔ stands for *E*.

A	E	F
G	J	L
N	O	W

Accidental Nails

Longest Fingernails on a Female
February 23, 2008

In 2008, Lee Redmond (USA) had the Longest Fingernails on a Female in the world. Almost 30 years after she started growing them, their combined lengths reached more than 28 feet (8.5 m). One thumbnail was nearly 3 feet (0.9 m) long!

It must have been hard to have such long nails. Redmond, however, did not mind. How did she do everyday things? "Very carefully," she always said. Somehow, Redmond went 30 years without breaking a single nail. She took good care of her nails. Every day, she soaked them in olive oil. She cleaned them with a toothbrush. Redmond was proud of her nails. They made her famous. Once, TV show producers offered her $100,000 to cut her nails on live TV. She said no.

Today, Redmond's nails are much shorter. On February 11, 2009, they broke when Redmond was in a car accident. Her nails had been her joy. Still, she knew she was lucky to be alive. In time, her body healed. She was still sad about her nails. But, she said, "There's more to life than nails." Redmond still holds the record, though, and will continue to until someone else grows longer nails than she had.

Word Bank

beak	brain	fang	hair	horn	*nail	shell	stomach
bladder	claw	feather	heart	liver	nerve	skin	whisker
blood	eye	fur	hoof	lung	scale	spleen	wool

● Hidden in the maze below is a word path. The words on the path name external animal parts that are composed of keratin, as skin and nails are. These words may be horizontal or vertical within the maze. The last letter in one word must join, but not overlap, the first letter in the next word, in any direction. Cross out the path words as you find them. Use the word bank to help you. Be careful! The word path contains only *external* body parts that are composed of keratin. You will not use all of the words in the word bank.

Start →

Finish →

t	e	y	e	x	d	o	o	l	b	l	s	a
*n	a	i	l	r	s	h	e	l	l	i	p	f
s	m	q	s	i	e	i	l	d	h	v	l	t
t	r	y	k	a	z	r	n	o	o	e	e	r*
o	e	x	i	h	d	a	k	o	r	r	e	e
m	d	i	n	r	u	f	w	l	n	h	n	h
a	d	e	b	v	e	l	a	c	s	e	i	t
c	a	v	e	p	h	u	l	t	o	a	a	a
h	l	r	a	h	o	k	c	j	g	r	r	e
d	b	e	k	w	o	o	l	c	b	t	b	f
l	g	n	u	l	f	w	h	i	s	k	e	r

Leggy Lady

Longest Legs on a Female
July 8, 2003

Svetlana Pankrotova (Russia) probably never wears hand-me-down jeans. That's because no one else's jeans will fit. Pankrotova has the longest legs in the world for a woman. She is 6 feet 5 inches (1.96 m) tall. Pankrotova's legs measure almost two-thirds of her entire height. Her legs are 4 feet 3.9 inches (1.32 m) long. That's taller than many children! Pankrotova was a regular 7-pound (3.18-kg) baby when she was born. But, as she grew taller, her legs grew longer and longer. Now an adult, Pankrotova is quite happy with her body. "I'm very fond of my legs," she says.

● Rearrange any or all of the letters in the phrase *WORLD'S LONGEST LEGS* to make new words using the letters. How long of a word can you create? Without using any of the actual words in the phrase (such as *legs*), write pairs of words on the lines below.

WORLD'S LONGEST LEGS

___ ___ two-letter word ___ ___

___ ___ ___ three-letter word ___ ___ ___

___ ___ ___ ___ four-letter word ___ ___ ___ ___

___ ___ ___ ___ ___ five-letter word ___ ___ ___ ___ ___

___ ___ ___ ___ ___ ___ six-letter word ___ ___ ___ ___ ___ ___

___ ___ ___ ___ ___ ___ ___ seven-letter word ___ ___ ___ ___ ___ ___ ___

___ ___ ___ ___ ___ ___ ___ ___ Longer words? ___ ___ ___ ___ ___ ___ ___ ___

Most Whole Blood Donated
December 24, 2009

Philip Baird (Australia) is known as a generous giver. He is not known for giving gifts of money though. He is known for giving gifts of blood! Baird has made more whole blood donations than anyone else in the world. He gave his 231st donation on Christmas Eve 2009 in Cessnock, Australia.

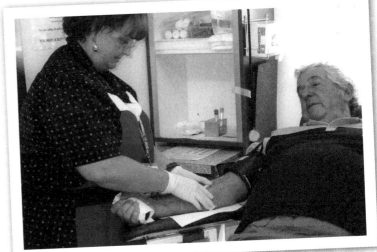

Baird first donated blood at the age of 19 in 1954. Since then, he has given blood every 12 weeks. In his lifetime, he has donated more than 210 pints (100 L)! Baird doesn't think of himself as a hero. He says that he just wants to help. He knows that hospitals badly need blood to save the lives of patients. Baird may not see himself as a hero, but those who have received his "gifts of life" would certainly disagree!

● After a person gives blood, the body produces new cells to replace what was lost. About how long does it take for the body to replace its red blood cells? To find out, first find the greatest common factor of each number pair. Write the number in the box. Then, use the code to write the matching letter for each factor you wrote.

18, 21   8, 10   36, 42   16, 24

☐   ☐   ☐   ☐

___   ___   ___   ___

27, 36   24, 28   12, 20   21, 35   35, 20

☐   ☐   ☐   ☐   ☐

___   ___   ___   ___   ___

Code
2 - o
3 - f
4 - e
5 - s
6 - u
7 - k
8 - r
9 - w

Ice Is Nice

Fastest Half Marathon Barefoot on Ice and Snow
January 26, 2007

Imagine running a course of 13 miles (about 20 km). That's the distance you would cover in a half marathon. Now, imagine running the course barefoot when it is covered with ice and snow. That's what Wim Hof (Netherlands) did. He ran in an area near the Arctic Circle. He finished the course in 2 hours, 16 minutes, 34 seconds. That was the fastest time ever for a half marathon run barefoot on ice and snow!

Hof's body can withstand very cold temperatures. In 2002, dressed only in a swimsuit, he dove under the ice at the North Pole. Another time, wearing only swimming trunks, he sat in a container of ice. He stayed there for more than an hour and came out perfectly healthy!

● Because of Hof's abilities, he is known by a certain name. To find out the name, read the clues. For each clue, cross out the ice cube with the matching answer. Then, rearrange the letters that are left to spell the name on the lines.

- $\frac{1}{3} + \frac{1}{3}$

- $\frac{4}{5} - \frac{1}{5}$

- $\frac{1}{2} + \frac{1}{4}$

- $\frac{7}{10} - \frac{3}{5}$

- $\frac{1}{8} + \frac{3}{4}$

- $\frac{2}{4} + \frac{4}{8}$

M $\frac{1}{3}$ S $\frac{2}{3}$ N $\frac{2}{5}$

E $\frac{3}{8}$ C $\frac{7}{10}$ L $\frac{3}{5}$

T $\frac{7}{8}$ A $\frac{1}{4}$ R $\frac{1}{10}$

M $\frac{1}{1}$ O $\frac{3}{4}$ I $\frac{1}{2}$

Hof is known as the ____ ____ ____ ____ ____ ____.

Shortest Teenager Living (Female)
September 6, 2009

Jyoti Amge (India) is an ordinary teenage girl. She goes to high school and loves fashion, music, and movies. She dreams of being a famous actress when she grows up. But, growing "up" doesn't mean getting taller. That's because Jyoti has achondroplasia, which is a type of dwarfism. Her arms and legs are very short. Jyoti is exactly 2 feet (0.61 m) tall. She is the shortest teenage girl in the world. And, if she still measures less than 28.6 inches (72.6 cm) on her 18th birthday in December 2011, she'll also hold the record for the shortest woman in the world! Jyoti loves being a celebrity. "I am proud of being small," she says. "I'm just the same as other people. I eat like you, dream like you. I don't feel any different."

Genes are the secret codes that tell our bodies how to grow and develop. We get genes from our parents, our grandparents, and our great-grandparents. Sometimes, genes change, or mutate. People with short-limbed dwarfism, like Jyoti, possess a gene that tells the body to stop bone growth too soon.

● The words to the right have been written using a secret alphabet-order code. The words refer to parts of our appearance that are determined by genes. Use the first answer to help you discover the code. Then, write your answers on the lines.

zwayzl

h e i g h t

esdw gj xwesdw

__ __ __ __   __ __   __ __ __ __ __

fgkw karw

__ __ __ __   __ __ __ __

fwwvk ydskkwk

__ __ __ __ __   __ __ __ __ __ __

kcaf ugdgj

__ __ __ __   __ __ __ __ __

kljsayzl lwwlz

__ __ __ __ __ __ __ __   __ __ __ __ __

wsjdgtwk

__ __ __ __ __ __ __ __

xjwucdwk

__ __ __ __ __ __ __ __

zsaj ugdgj

__ __ __ __   __ __ __ __ __

zwsv kzshw

__ __ __ __   __ __ __ __ __

Miracle Man

Highest Percentage of Burns to the Body Survived
February 15, 2004

Tony Yarijanian (USA) is a survivor. In 2004, Yarijanian was burned so badly that doctors thought he wouldn't survive. Ninety percent of his body was covered in third-degree burns. When his wife first saw him in the hospital, she insisted that the charred body on the bed was not her husband. But, it was. An accidental gas explosion had burned Yarijanian's entire face, hands, arms, legs, and most of his body. His lungs were also damaged from smoke inhalation.

Yarijanian was in a coma for three months. He endured more than 25 surgeries and 60 blood transfusions. But, he has recovered beyond everyone's expectations. Since the accident, Yarijanian has written a book about his experience. He is also the founder of an organization called Survivor's Hope. Yarijanian knows he is a lucky man. He thinks of himself not as a victim, but as a survivor. On those dark days when he thought he would never get better, his family encouraged him. "What's important is that you are here," they said. And, he knows they were right.

BEFORE

AFTER

● Using the clues below and the previous text, complete the crossword puzzle.

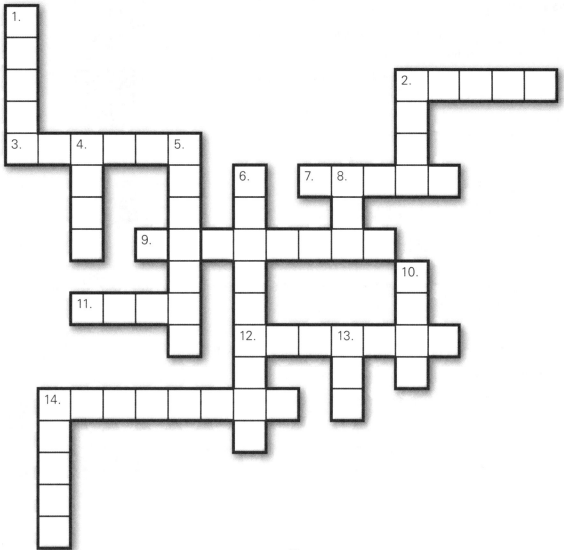

Across

2. Something Yarijanian received many transfusions of
3. Someone who treats patients
7. Opposite of unlucky
9. Place Yarijanian was treated
11. Where Yarijanian suffered the most burns
12. An operation
14. What Yarijanian considers himself

Down

1. The degree of burn that is the most severe
2. Something Yarijanian wrote about his experience
4. State of unconsciousness for a long time
5. To get better
6. Type of accident that caused the fire
8. Country where this accident occurred
10. What happens to skin when fire touches it
13. Substance that a broken dryer leaked, causing the fire
14. Something you may breathe in during a fire

CD-104546

Standing Tall

Shortest Living Man
October 14, 2010

Have you ever gotten a really special birthday gift? Khagendra Thapa Magar (Nepal) did. On his 18th birthday, he was given the Guinness World Records title of Shortest Living Man. Magar is 2 feet 2.41 inches (0.67 m) tall. He is only the height of an average toddler!

Magar was tiny even at birth. He weighed 1.3 pounds (600 g). He was so small that he could fit in the palm of his father's hand! Even now, he only weighs a little more than 12 pounds (5.5 kg). In spite of his small size, Magar is happy and proud. With his new title, he has become very popular in his country. He also has big plans for his future. He told reporters that he would one day like to marry and travel the world with his future wife.

● Magar's record height is about 26 inches. Here are some ways you can make the number 26.

You can add one plus sign to *1313* and get *13 + 13*.

You can add three plus signs to *5678* to get *5 + 6 + 7 + 8*.

● Add plus and minus signs to make other number sentences that equal 26.

1. Add one minus sign to 4115. _____

2. Add two minus signs to 3444. _____

3. Add two plus signs to 1196. _____

4. Make a number sentence with 2183. _____

5. Make a number sentence with 7524. _____

Record-Setting Hair

Longest Hair on a Female
May 8, 2004

When was your last haircut? For Xie Qiuping (China), it has been quite a while. That's because she has been growing her hair since she was 13 years old. That was in 1973, which was more than 30 years ago!

Xie Qiuping holds the record for having the Longest Hair on a Female. When her hair was measured in 2004, it was 18 feet 5 inches (5.6 m) long. Her hair is so long that when she stands, several feet of hair trail along the ground. When she sits, her hair flows all around her!

● Did you know that hair is the fastest-growing tissue in the human body? It grows on the scalp at a rate of about 1/2 inch (1.27 cm) every month. Use that fact to help you solve the problems below. (Hint: Make a list showing how long the person's hair is each month.)

1. Ginny just cut her hair. It is now 15 inches long. She plans to cut an inch off her hair every 6 months. How long will Ginny's hair be after she cuts her hair 1 year from now? _____

2. Nadia just got her hair trimmed. It is now 20 inches long. She plans to trim 3/4 inch off her hair every 2 months. How long will Nadia's hair be after 8 months? _____

CD-104546

Superstrong Woman

Most People Lifted and Thrown in Two Minutes (Female)
December 19, 2008

Aneta Florczyk (Poland) is a strong woman. She travels all over the world performing astonishing acts of strength. Florczyk started lifting weights at age 16. In 2008, the 26-year-old Florczyk achieved her second Guinness World Records record. Her first record had been for rolling metal frying pans into narrow cylinders. This record was for throwing people. In two minutes, Florczyk lifted and threw 12 full-grown men. The men weren't hurt though. They landed on a wrestling mat and bounced back for more action. Florczyk has appeared on several TV shows. She has lifted people, of course, but she has also rolled up frying pans, ice-skated, and danced. She has walked tightropes and modeled clothes. She has even been a contestant on a Polish quiz show.

● Many sports involve great strength. Florczyk started as a power lifter and then became a weight lifter. Now, she competes in another strength sport that requires power, speed, technique, and strength. Florczyk has been crowned this strength sport's world champion four times since 2003. Starting with **WEIGHT** lifting and **POWER** lifting, follow the directions, in order, to discover the unofficial name of Florczyk's current sport.

WEIGHT

Move the last 2 letters, in order, to in front of the W.

____ ____ ____ ____ ____ ____

Change WE to ON.

____ ____ ____ ____ ____ ____

Move the second vowel to the third position.

____ ____ ____ ____ ____ ____

Change H to S.

____ ____ ____ ____ ____ ____

Change the third letter to one that occurs nine positions later in the alphabet.

#1 ____ ____ ____ ____ ____ ____

POWER

Exchange the first two consonants.

____ ____ ____ ____ ____

Change E to the previous vowel in the alphabet

____ ____ ____ ____ ____

Replace the last letter with N.

____ ____ ____ ____ ____

Change PA to MA.

#2 ____ ____ ____ ____ ____

#1 + #2 = ____ ____ ____ ____ ____ ____ ____ ____ ____ ____ ____

Fingers and Friends

Most Fingers and Toes on a Living Person
October 19, 2005

Do you ever count on your fingers? When you get to 10, you have to sto[ ] and start all [ ]ver again, right? Pranamya Menaria and Devendra Harne (both India) do not. They can each count quite easi[ ]y to 12. And, if the[ ] were counting on their toe[ ], they would reach 13. That's because Pranamya and Devendra each have 12 fingers and 13 toes. *Polydactylism* (having extra fingers or toes) is not uncommon. One in 500 babies is born with this condition. Polydactylism is usuall[ ] inherited from the pare[ ]ts. It is passed [ ]own to the b[ ]bies through the parents' genes. The extra digits (*polydactyl*) are typi[ ]ally very small. Some[ ]imes fingers or toes are joined or webbed (*syndactyl*) to their neighbors. A surgeon can usuall[ ] remove or separate the extra or webbed digits. But, surgery is not essential. Having 12 fingers instead of 10 might be helpfu[ ], especiall[ ] in math class!

● Fill in the missing letters in the text above. Then, write them in order on the lines below to spell the name of the condition that includes **both** extra fingers or toes (polydactyl) **and** webbed fingers or toes (syndactyl).

___ ___ ___ ___ ___ ___ ___ ___ ___ ___ ___ ___ ___

A Well-Balanced Feat

Longest Duration Balancing on Four Fingers
November 9, 2008

Imagine a person "standing" upside down, balanced only on the fingers. Wang Weibao (China) did exactly that! Plus, he didn't use all of his fingers. He only used two fingers on one hand and two fingers on the other to support himself. He stayed that way for 19.23 seconds and set a world record.

To put weight on four fingers like Wang did takes incredible strength. Amazingly, the fingers themselves do not have any muscles. Instead, the muscles that control the fingers are in the forearms and the palms. Strong, slender "strings" called *tendons* connect the muscles to the fingers. The muscles move the fingers much like a puppeteer moves a puppet on a string!

● The numbers on the mats below show the time in seconds that some gymnasts can stay upright on their fingers. Look at the patterns and answer the questions.

1. | 1.50 | 1.95 | 2.40 | 2.85 | | | |

   What times do the next three gymnasts have? _____

2. | 4.75 | 4.65 | 4.45 | 4.15 | | | |

   What times do the next three gymnasts have? _____

3. | 7.15 | 8.26 | 9.48 | 10.81 | | | |

   What times do the next three gymnasts have? _____

CD-104546

A Russian Hercules

Heaviest Ship Pulled by Teeth
November 9, 2001

Omar Hanapiev (Russia) is called "Iron Teeth" for a good reason. This strongman uses his teeth to pull heavy objects. In 2001, he pulled a tanker weighing more than 1 million pounds (454 tonnes)! He pulled it a distance of 49 feet 2.4 inches (15 m). For that feat, he set the record for the Heaviest Ship Pulled by Teeth.

Hanapiev has had superstrong teeth from a young age. When he was 10 years old, he used his teeth to pull out nails from a board. He also used them to bend horseshoes. Besides ships, Hanapiev has pulled other vehicles with his teeth. This Russian Hercules has pulled a locomotive and even a passenger airplane!

● Find out the weight of the ship Hanapiev pulled. First, use the clues to write the numbers in the puzzle. Then, look at the number formed in the bold boxes. Read it from top to bottom. Write it on the lines to complete the sentence below.

1. The number of eggs in 9 dozen

2. The number of legs on 8 ants and 14 ladybugs

3. The number of inches in 10 yards

4. The number of feet on 546 children

5. The number of fingers on 810 pairs of hands

6. The number of days in 58 weeks

7. The number of tails on 56 dogs and 63 cats

The ship weighed ____ , ____ ____ ____ , ____ ____ ____ pounds.

CD-104546

Youngest Sword Swallower
July 21, 2006

Erik Kloeker (USA) considers himself a stunt artist. As soon as he started juggling at the age of 12, Kloeker knew that being a stunt artist was what he wanted to do with his life. By the time he was 16 years old, he was already attempting to swallow a sword. You can't just swallow any old sword to qualify as a sword swallower. The sword blade must be made of solid steel. It must be at least 15 inches (38 cm) long. And, it must be at least 1/2 inch (1.27 cm) wide. Three months before his 17th birthday, Erik swallowed a solid steel sword right up to the hilt. That performance earned him the title of the Youngest Sword Swallower ever. Erik is also one of the few people who can successfully juggle fire while swallowing a sword!

Sword swallowing has existed for about 4,000 years. Studying sword swallowers helped doctors create medical tests such as the endoscopy, where a tube with a camera is put down a patient's throat. *Sword swallowing can be dangerous and should only be attempted by trained performers.*

● S[w]ord s[w]allo[w]ing is just one of many circus tricks Erik has mastered. Below is a list of word groups. The words in each group are missing the same letter. Fill in the missing letters to discover the names of some other tricks that Erik performs in his circu[s] [s]ide[s]how.

[ ]uman block[ ][ ]ead   j[ ]ggling [ ]pside down

bullwh[ ]p art[ ]st   kn[ ]fe juggl[ ]ng

fir[ ][ ]ating   magi[ ] tri[ ]ks

g[ ]ass wa[ ]king   menta[ ] f[ ]oss

hum[ ]n d[ ]rtbo[ ]rd   str[ ]itj[ ]cket esc[ ]pe

Flight Delay

Longest Time Restraining Two Aircraft
July 7, 2007

How do you keep an airplane from taking off? Perhaps you can ask Chad Netherland (USA) for help. He holds the record for the Longest Time Restraining Two Aircraft. He set the record in 2007 at an airport in Superior, Wisconsin.

To perform his feat, Netherland strapped a large rubber band around each arm. The bands were connected to chains that were attached to two small airplanes. Netherland stood between the airplanes as they revved up and began to pull in opposite directions. He held his arms close to his body to keep the airplanes from moving forward. He was able to hold back the airplanes for a total of 1 minute, 0.6 seconds using only his arms!

● Imagine that the two airplanes in Netherland's feat flew off in opposite directions. Read the clues and solve the problem. (Hint: Look at the diagram and think about how far each airplane would be from its starting point after an hour.)

Plane A   Plane B

One airplane flew 15 miles per hour faster than the other airplane.

After one hour, the airplanes were 255 miles apart.

What was the speed of each airplane?

The faster airplane flew _____ miles per hour.

The slower airplane flew _____ miles per hour.

Talented on Tiptoes

Most Pirouettes on Pointe on the Head
December 21, 2006

Some couples like to sit close when they go on a date. When that date is to the Guangdong Military Acrobatic Troupe's production of *Swan Lake*, and the couple is Wei Baohua and Wu Zhengdan (both China), going on a date means more than sitting close together. It means standing on your husband's head on one foot, on tiptoe, while spinning around in a graceful pirouette. In 2006, the couple performed their beautiful routine on a Guinness World Records TV special. In her hard-toed pointe shoes, Wu raised one leg and completed three beautiful pirouettes on top of Wei's head. Wei and Wu are the only people in the world who are able to do this. "It took a lot of training," Wu says. "We spent half a year learning to hit the precise spot." They both have to be extremely careful. "Even a millimeter [off] can cause a fall."

Wei and Wu have trained from early childhood to be sports acrobats. They have won national and world championships. But, their acrobatic routines now include classical ballet moves. Are they acrobats, or are they ballet dancers? "I'm not sure," Wu says. "I can't leave the acrobatics world, but I'm not 100 percent in ballet." Acrobats or ballet dancers—it doesn't really matter. Their talent is what counts!

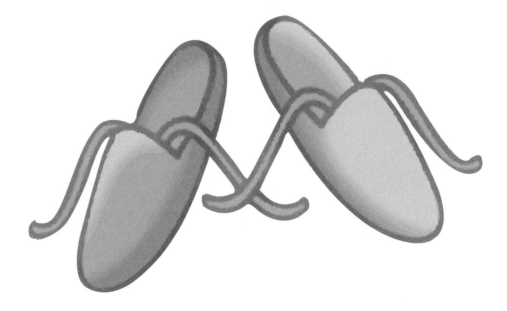

Acrobats learn four basic skills:

1. Tumbling

2. Flexibility

3. Handstand

4. ☐ ☐ ☐ ☐

● Using a color code, decode the following acrobatic stunts to determine this fourth acrobatic skill. Write your answer in the colorful boxes above.

A. foot juggli ☐ g

B. high wir ☐

C. pol ☐   limbi ☐ g

D.   o ☐ tortio ☐ ist

E. hum ☐ ☐   ☐ ☐ ☐ o ☐ b ☐ ll

F. pl ☐ t ☐   spi ☐ ☐ i ☐ g

G.   h ☐ ir st ☐   ki ☐ g h ☐ ☐ ☐ st ☐ ☐ ☐

H. hoop ☐ ivi ☐ g

I. bi   y   l ☐   p ☐ go ☐ ☐

A Pricey Cut

Most Expensive Haircut
October 29, 2007

How much do you think a good haircut should cost? Should it cost $50 or $100? Or, should it cost $16,420? That's how much hair stylist Stuart Phillips of London charged Beverley Lateo. That amount has earned the record for the world's Most Expensive Haircut.

Lateo is from Pisa, Italy. She could not find a hairdresser she liked in her country. She then heard about Stuart Phillips, a well-known British stylist. Lateo quickly booked an appointment. The cost of the pricey haircut included a limousine ride to and from the airport, a lunch or a dinner, a basket of hair products, and first-rate attention from Phillips. Was Lateo happy with the results? She must have been because she set up another appointment!

● Suppose a person has saved money for an expensive haircut. Luckily, the haircut costs only $1,000 instead of $16,420. The person has put the money into 5 piggy banks. The amounts are in whole-dollar amounts. Each amount can be written using only the number 8. Write the amounts on the banks. One has been done for you.

$88

CD-104546

© Carson-Dellosa

Time to Pack

Fastest Time to Enter a Suitcase
September 14, 2009

Leslie Tipton (USA) gives the phrase *pack your suitcase* a whole new meaning! Tipton is a contortionist. That is someone who can twist her body in unusual ways. In 2009, Tipton performed on a TV show. She twisted herself into a suitcase and then closed it in 5.43 seconds! That feat earned her a world record for the Fastest Time to Enter a Suitcase.

Tipton was born with a body that bends in amazing ways. She says that she can squish herself into a suitcase "just like you'd squish your clothes in"! She can also get herself out of a suitcase as quickly as she can get in. In fact, she holds the record for that feat too. Her fastest time to get in and out of a suitcase was 13.31 seconds!

● A contortionist is hiding in one of the four suitcases below. Figure out which suitcase she is in. Only one of the four sentences to the left of the suitcases is true. (Hint: Choose one suitcase at a time for the answer. If that suitcase is the answer, it will make three of the sentences false and one of the sentences true.)

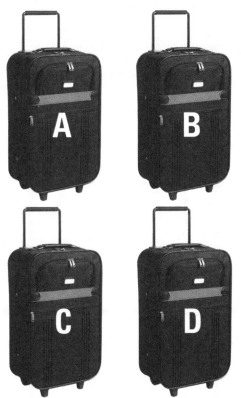

1. The contortionist is in suitcase B or C.

2. The contortionist is in suitcase A or D.

3. The contortionist is not in suitcase D.

4. The contortionist is in suitcase B.

The contortionist is in suitcase _____.

Eyes That Write

Most Words Blinked by a Published Author
October 5, 2007

For some people, writing isn't easy. For Chen Hung (China), it is even more difficult. Hung holds the world record for the Most Words Blinked by a Published Author. Hung has amyotrophic lateral sclerosis (ALS). He is completely paralyzed. But, he still manages to write. He dictates each word by blinking. At the time he set his 2007 world record, Hung had blinked an astonishing 190,185 words, producing four published books. He has published more since then.

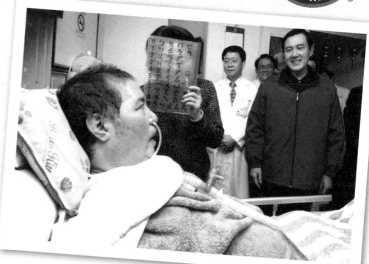

Communication through blinking is not easy, especially in the Chinese language. Hung uses a *Bopomofo* board that connects symbols to Chinese characters. Multiple symbols form one character. Multiple characters form one word. Multiple words form one sentence. Hung's wife translates his blinks by selecting the right symbols on the board. She repeats every sound to make sure it is correct. A single sentence may take 10 minutes to create.

● Below are the titles of some of Hung's blinked books. Several of the words have been translated for you. The remaining words remain in their single-letter state. Using the letters in the boxes, fill in the missing words.

| B EEE N T W | _ _ _ _ _ _ _ Blinks |

| _ _ _ _ _ Life _ _ _ _ _ _ Blinks | B EEEE F L N OO R T V W |

| AAA D G H I N O R R S | _ _ _ _ _ as _ Rock and _ _ _ _ _ _ _ _ _ _ Bird |

| I Saw _ _ _ _ _ _ _ _ | A B EE G I R T |

| AA E F H I N R S T W | _ _ Easy _ _ _ _ _ in Shallow _ _ _ _ _ _ |

CD-104546

"Truck" Wrestling

Heaviest Truck Pulled by One Arm
September 26, 2010

René Richter (Czech Republic) has taken arm wrestling to a whole new level. In arm wrestling, two people face each other across a table. They each rest an elbow on the table and grip the opponent's hand. Then, they each try to push the other person's hand down on the table. Richter used this same arm wrestling move, but he competed against a truck!

With his elbow resting on a table, Richter pulled on a strap. The strap was attached to a truck that weighed a whopping 19,227.8 pounds (8,721.6 kg)! Richter pushed down with his arm, and slowly the truck moved. Richter set a new record for the Heaviest Truck Pulled by One Arm!

● **Learn more facts about strongman Richter. Follow the directions on the trucks in order. Then, write the answers on the lines.**

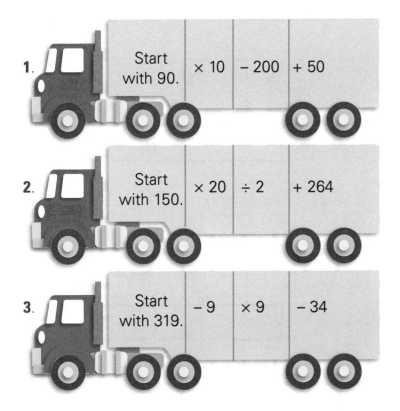

1. Start with 90. | × 10 | − 200 | + 50

Richter has lifted _____ pounds with one hand.

2. Start with 150. | × 20 | ÷ 2 | + 264

Richter has lifted _____ pounds with both hands.

3. Start with 319. | − 9 | × 9 | − 34

Richter has lifted _____ pounds on his back.

Bearded Liftoff!

Heaviest Weight Lifted by a Human Beard
September 16, 2007

Most strongmen lift weights with their hands and arms. Antanas Kontrimas (Lithuania) uses his beard! In 2005, he lifted a woman who weighed 138 pounds (62.6 kg). The woman wore a strap around her body. Kontrimas wrapped his beard around the strap and lifted her about 4 inches (10.16 cm) off the ground!

In 2007, he attempted to beat his own record. This time, he used his beard to lift a woman who weighed 139.33 pounds (63.2 kg). That feat set a new record for the Heaviest Weight Lifted by a Human Beard. Kontrimas says he has lifted even heavier weights with his beard. Perhaps he'll prove that by setting yet another world record in the future.

● Imagine that Kontrimas is going to lift the boards below. Stacked on the boards are different-shaped weights. The weight on one half equals the weight on the other half. How many rectangles will it take to balance the last board? (Hint: Because a triangle and a rectangle balance a square, they must also balance a circle.)

1.

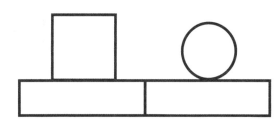

2.

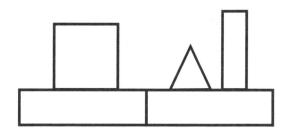

3.

4.

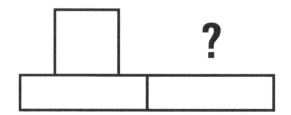

It will take _____ rectangles to balance the square.

CD-104546

Funny Faces

Most Gurning World Championships Wins (Male)

Wouldn't it be great to win a world championship for making silly faces? Tommy Mattinson (UK) thinks so. Mattinson is the only man to have won the Gurning World Championships 12 times! Gurning is the art of making faces. Mattinson is an expert at transforming his face to look surprised, happy, sad, or just plain silly. Gurners aren't allowed to use their hands to move any part of their heads. The Gurning World Championships titles are awarded by Egremont Crab Fair and Sports in England. This fair has been around for almost 800 years. Mattinson learned about gurning from his father, who had won championships almost as many times as Mattinson. Making faces may sound easy. But, to win more championships, Mattinson knows that he must keep practicing.

● Making a small change in your facial expression can make a big change in how people see you. It's the same for words. One different letter can make an entirely different word. Each word below is really the name of a facial expression or a movement in disguise. Change the boxed letter in each word to discover the new facial or movement word. Use the letters scattered across the page.

t̲eam ___ eam	b̲urrow ___ urrow	gla d̲ e gla ___ e	s h̲ irk s ___ irk
mo r̲ e mo ___ e	f l̲ own f ___ own	gri p̲ gri ___	smi t̲ e smi ___ e
po s̲ t po ___ t	d̲ eer ___ eer	su n̲ k su ___ k	s h̲ eer s ___ eer

CD-104546

A Piping-Hot Path of Plates

Longest Distance Walking Over Hot Plates
April 18, 2009

Rolf Iven (Germany) likes to get himself into hot situations. That's because he sets world records by walking barefoot across a path of hot plates! In 2009, he performed in Milan, Italy. He covered 75 feet 1 inch (22.90 m) on a piping-hot path. That was the farthest anyone had ever walked on a path of hot plates.

All of the hot plates on Iven's path were very hot. Their temperatures ranged from 266°F to 302°F (130°C to 150°C). Those temperatures are hot enough to make water boil! Iven didn't seem to mind though. In fact, he looked quite "cool" while walking his way into the record books!

● Imagine that you are going to make a rectangular walkway with 24 hot plates. Each plate sits in the middle of a 1-foot-square surface.

Example

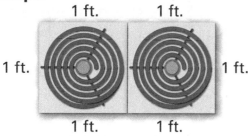

The perimeter of this rectangle is 6 feet.

1. How can you arrange the squares so that your walkway has the largest perimeter possible? (The perimeter is the distance around a shape.) _____

   _____

   What will its perimeter be? _____

2. How can you arrange the squares so that your walkway has the smallest perimeter possible?

   _____

   _____

   What will its perimeter be? _____

Ready, Pick Up, Go!

Fastest 20 Meters Carrying 300 Kilograms on the Shoulders
April 18, 2009

Agris Kazelniks (Latvia) lifts heavy weights, and then he runs with them! In 2009, he hoisted 661 pounds 5.4 ounces (330 kg) on his shoulders. He carried the weight a distance of 65 feet 7.32 inches (20 m). He did all of that in just 11.4 seconds and set a world record for the Fastest 20 Meters Carrying 300 Kilograms on the Shoulders.

Kazelniks trains hard for strongman competitions. He trains with weights and other equipment. Yet, this husky fellow has a soft side to him. He says that his favorite movie is about Winnie the Pooh. He has a surprising nickname too. It's Mazinais, and it means "little one"!

● Below are heavy metal weights placed on steps. The steps weigh 31 pounds. The weights are 30, 40, 50, 60, 70, 80, 90, 100, and 110 pounds. The total weight, including the steps, equals the amount that Kazelniks carried on his shoulders. Arrange the numbers so that the sum in each horizontal, vertical, and diagonal row is the same. Three of the weights have been filled in for you.

Don't Drop That Ball!

Most Consecutive Foot-Juggling Flips
September 19, 2007

What do you picture when you hear the word *juggle*? If you're like most people, you probably see clowns tossing and catching balls with their hands. When acrobats hear the word *juggle*, they probably imagine much more than that—dancing desk drawers, prancing plates, flying fire torches, and even bodies! Hou Yanan and Jiang Tiantian hold the record for the Most Consecutive Foot-Juggling Flips with 90. They are members of the Wuqiao County Acrobatic Group (China). What is so amazing about this record is that the juggler, Yanan, doesn't stand and juggle using her hands. She lies on her back and juggles with her feet. And, she's not juggling balls, she's juggling her teammate. Not only does Tiantian get tossed in the air 90 times in a row, but she also does 90 perfect flips while she's at it. Their timing is perfect—juggle-flip, juggle-flip, juggle-flip . . .

Foot juggling is an ancient acrobatic art. Acrobatics became extremely popular in China about 2,500 years ago. The emperors enjoyed performances, so more and more people performed. The hot spot of Chinese acrobatics was in Wuqiao (pronounced "oo-chow") County. Family troupes developed new stunts and passed these down through the generations. Wuqiao County is still home to many talented acrobats.

- On the following page are seven word puzzles. These puzzles are in the shape of foot jugglers. Each puzzle reads from top to bottom and from left to right. For each puzzle, the last letter in the first vertical word is the same as the first letter in the horizontal word; the last letter in the second vertical word is the same as the last letter in the horizontal word. All first and last letters have been filled in for you. All of the words can be found in the passage above. Be careful! You may have to change a word to its singular form or spell out a number.

- When you have completed the puzzles on the next page, write the numbered letters in order on the lines below to discover the traditional name for a Chinese juggling extravaganza.

___ ___ ___ ___ ___ ___   ___ ___ ___ ___ ___ ___ ___ ___ ___ ___ ___

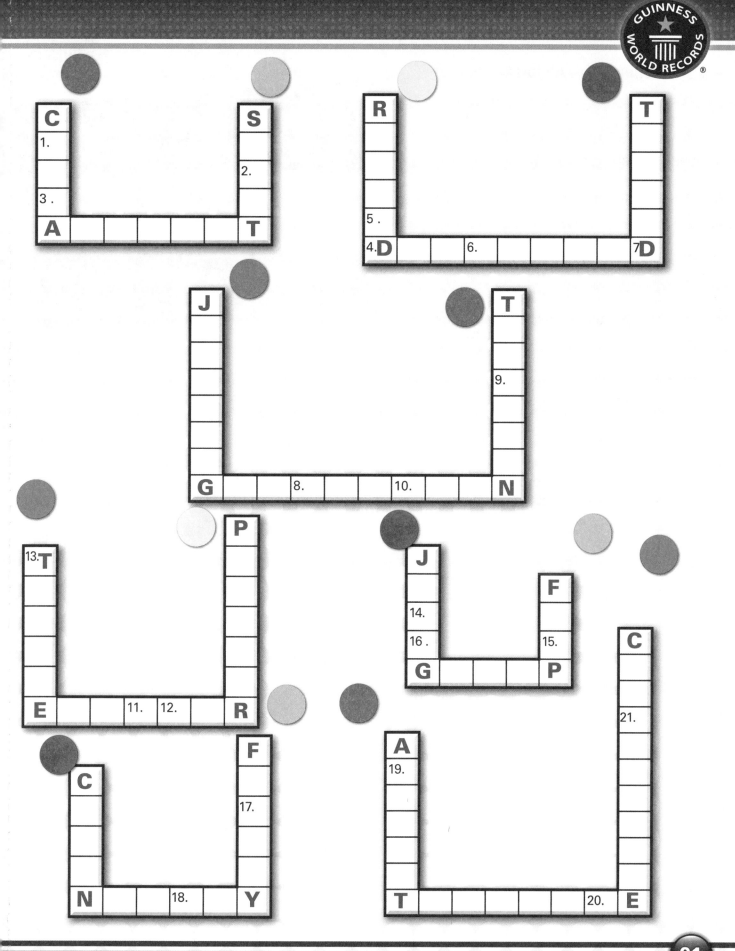

One in Four

Most Siblings with Albinism

It's not just old people who have white hair. If you're one of the 400,000 people in the world with albinism, you may too. In the 1920s, the oldest four children of the Sesler family (USA) were born with albinism. In the 1980s in another family, all four Gaulet children (Canada) were born with albinism. People with albinism usually have white hair and skin and blue eyes, no matter what their ethnic background. Because of the lack of coloring behind their eyes, people with albinism have poor eyesight. The word *albino* was historically used to name people with albinism. But, as Josh Gaulet explains, "I'm a guy with a vision impairment. I am not the impairment itself." The term *albino* is now outdated. If a person has white hair, pale skin, and poor vision, he may be a person with *albinism*.

The Gaulet Siblings

● Albinism is a genetic condition. You may not have the gene, you may carry the gene, or you may actually have albinism. If two parents carry the gene, like the Seslers, one in four of their children would probably have albinism. In the following word sets, one word in every set of four is a little different. For each set, circle which word you think is unique. Write your reason on the lines. There may be more than one correct answer.

Set 1 _____
cheek _____
chin _____
elbow _____
eyes _____

Set 2 _____
brown _____
green _____
white _____
yellow _____

Set 3 _____
five _____
one _____
three _____
two _____

Set 4 _____
freckle _____
mole _____
skin _____
wart _____

Set 5 _____
brother _____
father _____
mother _____
parent _____

Breaking Records for a Better World

Longest Continuous Crawl
May 18–19, 2001

Arulanantham Suresh Joachim (Australia) is on a mission. He wants to raise awareness, as well as money, to help needy children. To reach his goal, Joachim performs record-breaking feats. One was the world's Longest Continuous Crawl. Joachim kept his knees in constant contact with the ground as he crawled along an outdoor track. He covered 35.18 miles (56.62 km) and completed 2,500 laps!

Joachim was born in Sri Lanka, an island country near India. He has seen the effects of poverty and violence. Joachim hopes that he can do his part to help make the world a better place.

● Find out how many records Joachim hopes to set in just eight years. Use the ordered pairs to draw points on the grid. Connect the points with straight lines as shown by the arrows. The first line has been drawn for you. Then, use the number that appears to complete the sentence.

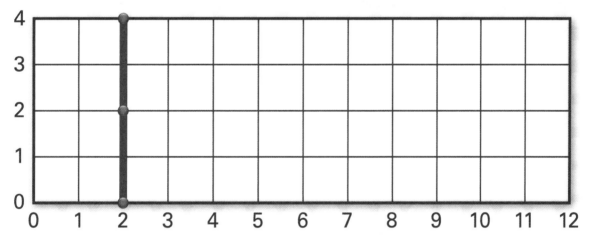

(2,4) ➡ (2,2) ➡ (2,0)
(6,4) ➡ (4,4) ➡ (4,2) ➡ (6,2)
(10,4) ➡ (8,4) ➡ (8,2) ➡ (8,0)
(6,2) ➡ (6,0) ➡ (4,0)
(10,4) ➡ (10,0) ➡ (8,0)

Joachim hopes to set _____ records in eight years.

Answer Key

Page 6

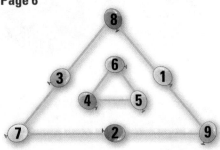

Page 7
1. 19; 2. 4; 3. 8; 4. 12

Page 8
Answers will vary but may include
1. American flag; 2. tiger; 3. sun in sky;
4. zebra sticking out tongue; 5. crocodile in water; 6. brown-and-white cat.

Page 9
People who are different still have dignity. I am very proud to be who I am.

Page 10

Page 11
BUBBLE GUM; ULE GUM; CLE GCM; GCMCLE; CGMCLE; CHMCLE; CHICLE

Page 12
Tony, Kevin, Carlos, Janelle

Page 13
150

Page 14
pudding; cheese; beet; waffle; egg; jelly; cookie; apple; carrot; porridge; butter; lettuce

Page 15
before work; answer later; fill yours; cry loudly; close slowly; walk under; frown seldom; sit low; give many; learn well; dry night; old man

Page 16
five minutes

Page 17
1. the 23rd; 2. 10 times; 3. 3 weeks or 21 days later

Pages 18–19
congresses

Page 20
Across: 3. letters; 6. fastest; 7. India; 8. keys
Down: 1. words; 2. minute; 4. record; 5. alphabet; 6. fingers

Page 21
Justin–dinosaur; Lee–dog; Kori–butterfly; Tracy–unicorn

Page 22
ears; teeth; one hand

Page 23
1. 3 adults, 3 children; 2. 3 adults, 5 children; 3. 4 adults, 6 children

Page 24
1. Shane–16, Tyesha–8, Kelly–4; 2. 32

Page 25
Hungarian; German; French; Italian; Filipino; Portuguese; Indonesian; Japanese; Maltese; Norwegian

Page 26
1. 1, 21; 2. 0, 11

Page 27
puts; inside; Most; live; whole; more; started; always; thrilling; cannot; tame; still; all; few; ends; lost

Pages 28–29
prehensile; flop; riser; heat; pins; king; smile

Page 30
spoon; spook; shook; shock; stock; stick

Page 31
1. 74, 84, 96, 110 (+2, +4, +6, +8, . . .), 110; 2. 210, 180, 160, 150 (–70, –60, –50, –40, . . .), 150; 3. 205, 230, 225, 250 (+25, –5, +25, –5), 250

Page 32
1. VEHICLE; 2. WEIGHT; 3. HOUSE

Page 33
ILLUSION

Page 34

Page 35
Delightful False Teeth

Page 36
1. golf ball; 2. grapefruit

Page 37
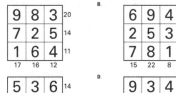

Page 38
Answers will vary.
dad; race car; radar; kayak; level; bib/did; did/bib; mom/wow/pop; wow/mom/pop; pup/mum

Page 39
16

Page 40
chimp; eater; mouth; stone; sloth; twine; truth; where

Page 41
jet

Page 42
fastest; buttons; player; melody; hand; instrument; air; presses; fold a map

Page 43
wide; hide; cry; fly; Rome; home; wide; pride; Jay; say; fine; mine

Page 44
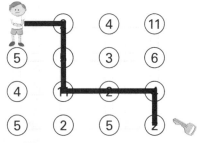

Page 45
Hayley–45; Jose–55; Kelsey–60

Page 46
Answers will vary but may include
Loud: scream; bellow; cry; exclaim; holler; roar; shout; wail; yell
Soft: whisper; croak; grumble; hiss; murmur; peep; sigh; twitter; whimper

Page 47
split; high chair; tuck; needle; pyramid; cradle; scorpion; thunder

CD-104546

Page 48

1. 22 (8 blocks high, 7 blocks to the left, and 7 blocks to the right); 2. The number of blocks in the tower equals the number of feet in height. The blocks to the left and right each have one less than the blocks in the tower. (Example: For a 12-foot tower, add 12 + 11 + 11.)

Page 49

chomp; gnaw; shred; eat; grind; crush; mash; bite; chew; masticate

Page 50

THE RUBBERBOY

Page 51

SHE WANTS TO BE A TEACHER.

Page 52

Answers will vary but may include banker/Vincent; butcher/Dubrawski; carpenter/Atwood; cook/Campana; doctor/Healey; firefighter/Cashman; jeweler/Harrington; logger/Deforest; mechanic/Carmignani; meteorologist/ Weatherby; secretary/Stapleton; skater/ Brinkman; teacher/Knowlton; veterinarian/ Cataldo; zookeeper/Wilder.

Page 53

1. 320; 2. 180; 3. 150; 4. 360; 5. 160; 6. 250; 7. 420; 8. 350; 9. 240; circus

Pages 54–55

second; minute; hour; day; week; month; year; decade; century; millennium; supercentenarian

Page 56

blond, red, black, brown, white

Page 57

press; top roll; hook

Page 58

2. 5,116; The product of the first and last digits equals the middle two digits.
3. 6,143; The first digit is the sum of the last three digits. 4. 3,339; The last digit is the product of the first three digits.

Page 59

100

Page 60

Now I am working to set new records with basketballs, footballs, and fruit.

Page 61

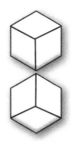

Page 62

his father

Page 63

ANGOLAN JAW OF AWE

Pages 64–65

t	e	y	e	x	d	o	o	l	b	l	s	a
n	a	i	l	r	s	h	e	l	l	i	p	f
s	m	q	s	l	e	i	l	d	h	v	l	t
t	r	y	k	a	z	r	n	o	o	e	e	r
o	e	x	i	h	d	a	k	o	r	r	e	e
m	d	i	n	r	u	f	w	l	n	h	n	h
a	d	e	b	v	e	l	a	c	s	e	i	t
c	a	v	e	p	h	u	l	t	o	a	a	a
h	l	r	a	h	o	k	c	j	g	r	r	e
d	b	e	k	w	o	o	l	c	b	t	b	f
l	g	n	u	l		w	h	i	s	k	e	r

Page 66

Answers will vary but may include to/ we; set/row; door/grew; notes/drown; longer/rented; streets/greeted; wordless; strongest.

Page 67

3, 2, 6, 8; 9, 4, 4, 7, 5; four weeks

Page 68

ICEMAN

Page 69

height; male or female; nose size; needs glasses; skin color; straight teeth; earlobes; freckles; hair color; head shape

Pages 70–71

Across: 2. blood; 3. doctor; 7. lucky; 9. hospital; 11. face; 12. surgery; 14. survivor
Down: 1. third; 2. book; 4. coma; 5. recover; 6. explosion; 8. USA; 10. burn 13. gas; 14. smoke

Page 72

1. 41 – 15; 2. 34 – 4 – 4; 3. 1 + 19 + 6; 4. 21 + 8 – 3; 5. 7 – 5 + 24

Page 73

1. 19 inches (The hair will grow 3 inches in 6 months; when 1 inch is cut, it will be 17 inches. The hair will grow another 3 inches in the next 6 months; when 1 inch is cut, it will be 19 inches.)

2. 21 inches (Every 2 months, the hair grows 1 inch, but 3/4 inch is cut off. That means the hair will be only 1/4 inch longer every 2 months. After 8 months, the hair will be 1 inch longer [1/4 x 4].)

Page 74

STRONGWOMAN

Page 75

stop; over; easily; they; toes; usually; parents; down; babies; typically; sometimes; usually; helpful; especially; polysyndactyly

Page 76

1. 3.30, 3.75, 4.20 (+0.45 each time); 2. 3.75, 3.25, 2.65 (–0.10, –0.20, –0.30, etc.); 3. 12.25, 13.80, 15.46 (+1.11, +1.22, +1.33, etc.)

Page 77

1,269,861

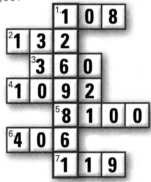

Page 78

human blockhead; bullwhip artist; fire eating; glass walking; human dartboard; juggling upside down; knife juggling; magic tricks; mental floss; straitjacket escape

Page 79

135, 120

Pages 80–81

dance; A. foot juggling; B. high wire; C. pole climbing; D. contortionist; E. human cannonball; F. plate spinning; G. chair stacking handstand; H. hoop diving; I. bicycle pagoda

CD-104546

Answer Key

Page 82

The five amounts are $88, $888, $8, $8, and $8.

Page 83

The contortionist is in suitcase D.

Page 84

Answers will vary but may include Between Blinks; Love for Life Between Blinks; Hard as a Rock and Soaring Bird; I Saw a Big Tree; An Easy Fish in Shallow Water.

Page 85

1. 750; 2. 1,764; 3. 2,756

Page 86

3 rectangles (Because 1 triangle and 1 rectangle balance a square, they will also balance a circle (based on board 1). Then, you know that 2 triangles and 2 rectangles will balance 2 circles. That means 2 triangles and 2 rectangles equal 3 triangles (based on board 3). That means 2 rectangles equal 1 triangle. If you replace the triangle in board 2 with 2 rectangles, you will get 3 rectangles balancing the square.)

Page 87

beam; mope; pout; furrow; frown; leer; glare; grin; sulk; smirk; smile; sneer

Page 88

1. Make a 1 x 24 rectangle/perimeter – 50 ft.; 2. Make a 4 x 6 rectangle/ perimeter – 20 ft.

Page 89

top row–100, 30, 80; middle row–50, 70, 90; bottom row–60, 110, 40

Pages 90–91

hundred entertainments; China/acrobat/ stunt; record/developed/tossed; juggling/ generation/Tiantian; troupe/emperor/ popular; Jiang/group/flip; clown/ninety/ family; ancient/teammate/consecutive

Page 92

Answers will vary.

Page 93

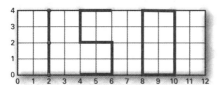